THE SECRET SCIENCE OF SPORTS

THE SECRET SCIENCE OF SPORTS

THE MATH, PHYSICS, AND MECHANICAL ENGINEERING BEHIND EVERY GRAND SLAM, TRIPLE AXEL, AND PENALTY KICK

JENNIFER SWANSON
ILLUSTRATED BY LAURÈNE BOGLIO

BLACK DOG
& LEVENTHAL
PUBLISHERS
NEW YORK

Black Dog & Leventhal Publishers
Hachette Book Group
1290 Avenue of the Americas
New York, NY 10104

www.hachettebookgroup.com
www.blackdogandleventhal.com

First Edition: July 2021

Black Dog & Leventhal Publishers is an imprint of Perseus Books, LLC,
a subsidiary of Hachette Book Group, Inc. The Black Dog & Leventhal Publishers
name and logo are trademarks of Hachette Book Group, Inc.

The publisher is not responsible for websites (or their content) that are not owned by the publisher.

The Hachette Speakers Bureau provides a wide range of authors for speaking events.
To find out more, go to www.HachetteSpeakersBureau.com or call (866) 376-6591.

Print book interior design by Katie Benezra.

Library of Congress Cataloging-in-Publication Data
Names: Swanson, Jennifer, author.
Title: The secret science of sports : the math, physics, and mechanical engineering behind every grand slam, triple axel, and penalty kick / Jennifer Swanson.
Description: First edition. | New York : Black Dog & Leventhal, 2021. | Includes bibliographical references and index. | Audience: Ages 8–12 | Summary: "For kids ages 8 to 12, The Science of Sports combines kid-friendly language and vibrant, original illustrations to show how principles of STEM are behind every soccer kick, slap shot, home run, and slam dunk"—Provided by publisher.
Identifiers: LCCN 2020035793 (print) | LCCN 2020035794 (ebook) |
ISBN 9780762473038 (trade paperback) | ISBN 9780762473014 (ebook) | 9781549108501 (audiobook)
Subjects: LCSH: Sports sciences—Juvenile literature.
Classification: LCC GV558 .S93 2021 (print) | LCC GV558 (ebook) | DDC 796.01/5—dc23
LC record available at https://lccn.loc.gov/2020035793
LC ebook record available at https://lccn.loc.gov/2020035794

ISBNs: 978-0-7624-7303-8 (trade paperback); 978-0-7624-7302-1 (hardcover); 978-0-7624-7301-4 (ebook)

Printed in China

APS

10 9 8 7 6 5 4 3 2 1

To my brothers Steve, Ted, and Jeff,
who I spent many fun hours with in the
backyard playing every sport we could think
of, and even ones we thought up.

CONTENTS

CHAPTER 3:
ENGINEERING A WIN............ 87

CHAPTER 4:
MATH + SPORTS = KNOWLEDGE 129

INTRODUCTION

IF YOU PICKED up this book, it's probably because you like sports. Maybe you want to see if it has tips for how to improve your game (it does), or how to become more fit (it has that, too), or just because you want to learn more about different types of sports (also there). But wait, the title says, "the Science of Sports." That means this book also teaches you about science. Why does a sports book have science in it? Those two subjects seem so different. It's not as if sitting in a science class can teach you more about your sport than practicing it. Actually, it can. Does that surprise you? It shouldn't. Science and, in particular, STEM topics (Science, Technology, Engineering, and Math) can teach you tons of stuff about how to get better at sports.

While many people don't realize it, *every* sport involves a bit of each of those topics. In fact, if you play sports you are already doing STEM, every time you play! Playing sports and science go together like, well, a bat and a ball, or a tennis ball and a racket, or a hockey puck and a stick...You get the idea. Understanding science helps you with sports. (Shhh...don't tell anyone. That's the secret part.) Put it this way: Do you throw a ball? That's physics. Do you play on a team? That

falls into the neuroscience category (science of the brain). Do you keep statistics about how many times you catch a football or make a basket? That's math. And if you wear any type of equipment—a helmet, running shoes, cleats, shoulder or knee pads—those were designed using engineering. That's right! STEM = Sports. Bet you thought science class was just for learning about biology and chemistry. (Hint: Those are also found in sports.)

So, this is a book about STEM and Sports? Hold on. Is it boring? Well, you might think that a book about STEM isn't exactly exciting. But you would be WRONG. The science, technology, engineering, and math of SPORTS is actually pretty cool, and very interesting, too.

Besides being cool, this book *may* help you get better at sports. It's true. The information in this book, combined with some practice, could help you to sink more free throws, hit a ball farther, or even cut a few seconds off your overall performance time. Why not give it a shot? (But not a kick or a throw. Books don't like that.)

So, keep reading and learn how to get your best game on with the science of sports!

CHAPTER 1

PUTTING THE SCIENCE IN SPORTS

SCIENCE PLAYS SUCH a big part in sports, it's hard to pick which topics to discuss. This chapter will deal with body science, brain science, and fitness and nutrition science. These are biological and life sciences and seemed to be the ones most people have questions about. But, of course, there are many more science aspects of sports. If you don't see something here, go look it up!

BODY SCIENCE

Let's start with body science. Can *anyone* play *any* sport? The quick answer is yes. If you have determination to learn, understand, and spend lots of time practicing, you can play any sport you want. The question that might be a better one to ask is: Do certain physical traits (big hands, big muscles, speed, agility) help you perform better at a particular sport? Yes, they can. Below is an illustration that might give you an idea of what physical traits help with which sports. Basically, this illustration says that athletes who excel at basketball,

wrestling, or weight lifting tend to be taller and have large muscular bodies. A world-class gymnast, runner, or boxer, however, might be shorter and have a smaller body.

Why are these body types considered to be the preferred ones for each sport? It comes down to physics. A larger person may have more energy and can push people away from them with more force, like in football or wrestling. They may be able to hit the volleyball or tennis ball harder across the net. Perhaps their force of pulling on the oar is so great that it propels the boat farther across the water, as in rowing or crew. But larger people also have to deal with more drag, that is, the force acting against them when they move through a fluid, such as air or water.

Smaller people are going to have less drag. That makes sense, doesn't it? Their bodies are more petite, so they would have to push through a lot less air or water as they move. That is one reason why many world-class runners are small and lean. They can

WHAT IS DRAG?

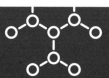

DRAG IS THE force you feel pushing back on you as you move through water or air. (Did you know air is a fluid? It is.) Drag acts in the opposite direction of your movement. Have you ever been in a swimming pool and just tried to walk through the water? It takes a lot more effort than walking on land, doesn't it? What you are feeling is drag. Why is drag greater in the water than in air? Water is more dense, or thicker, than air. Of course, if you are walking on a windy day, you will feel more drag than on a normal day. That is because the air is rushing past you and it requires more energy to push through it. You may even find yourself leaning into the wind, or bending over.

This is exactly what athletes do. Cyclists hunch over their bikes to reduce drag and make themselves go faster. Drag plays a huge part in how well an athlete performs! And you thought physics was just for kids who loved science. ☺

run faster because the force of drag doesn't slow them down as much as it would a larger person.

Does that mean a smaller person isn't in as great a shape as a larger athlete with more muscles? Not at all. Think about world-class gymnast Simone Biles. She is only four foot eight, and yet she can catapult herself extremely high into the air. That takes a lot of power! Simone is definitely a strong athlete who is in tip-top shape.

This is not to say that bigger people can't be in excellent physical shape, too. They totally can. The size of your body isn't a determining factor in whether or not you are in great physical shape.

Remember one thing: While body science does play a part in performance, it is not everything. If you are a long, lean person, you can still be an excellent rower or football player. Shorter, muscular people can also be fantastic swimmers and volleyball players. There are exceptions to every "rule" listed here.

You've already learned that size can give you an advantage in a particular sport. The real question is: Can you change your body to make it fit the sport you want to play? Sort of. You can't make yourself taller, but you could work out a lot to build muscle. In fact, athletes who work out every day for long periods of time do see physical changes in their bodies. A weight lifter will have big, strong muscles from lifting weights all the time. Runners may have long, lean muscle from running and burning fat all the time. Skaters will have really strong legs from pushing off the ice or the ground. Basketball players may be able to jump higher than most people because of their practice shooting baskets. Sometimes you can tell what type of athlete a person is by looking at them, but not always.

For example, swimmers tend to have higher body fat than other athletes. Why? The extra fat makes them more buoyant, which helps them float more easily in water. If they float more easily, then they need less power to propel themselves through the water.

WHAT IS BODY FAT?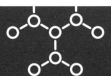

BODY FAT? Is that bad? Nope. Everyone needs to have some fat in their body to survive. Fat keeps your body warm. It supports and acts like a cushion for your internal organs. You know, your stomach, liver, intestines, etc. Fat also is your food storage system. If you get low on energy, your body burns fat to give you more. Finally, did you know that your brain is 60 percent fat? It is! Fat keeps your brain working well. So, when we talk about body fat, it's as a way to show you how fit you are, yes, but the goal is never to have zero percent body fat. Without any body fat you would be very sick. Even elite athletes need to have at least 3 percent body fat if they are men, and 12 percent body fat if they are women.

So, what is body fat? Think of it this way, when you step on a scale, you get your weight. Right? Say you weigh 70 lbs (31.75 kg). That number is great, but it doesn't tell you anything about how your body is made up. Is 70 percent of that weight muscle and organ tissue and 30 percent body fat?

Or is it more like 85 percent is muscle tissue and 15 percent body fat? If you are an athlete, your goal is to have more muscle tissue and less body fat.

How do you calculate your body fat? Doctors use something called the BMI—body mass index. You can find out your own BMI by using this simple calculation from the National Institutes of Health (NIH):

STEP 1: Weigh yourself in pounds (lbs).

STEP 2: Measure your height in inches.

STEP 3: Square your height, meaning if your height is 55 inches, you take 55^2, or multiply 55 × 55.

STEP 4: Divide your weight by your height squared.

STEP 5: Multiply the answer by 703.

> **EXAMPLE:**
> Your weight is 70 lbs.
> Your height is 55 inches or 55^2 or 55 × 55 = 3025
> Calculate: 70 ÷ 3025 = 0.0231 × 703 = 16.3 is your BMI

BMI RANGE FOR ADULTS:

18.5 to 24.9 is normal
25.0 to 29.9 is overweight
30.0 + is obese

The BMI for children is different because it compares kids to other kids of their same ages. For accuracy, ask your doctor.

Can you change your BMI? Sure. You can work out to change your BMI. Practicing your sport helps a lot with that. There are also exercises you can do to improve your speed, your agility (how well you can zigzag and dodge things), and even how high you jump. All those traits will definitely help improve your performance in sports. But in the long run, performance is not about your size or shape; it's all about how hard you work and your dedication to succeed.

BIG OR SMALL?

Let's see how size works in an actual sport. If you were asked to imagine a football player, what would that player look like? Do you see a fairly tall, large man, with lots of muscles? One who is a little smaller, and leaner, who can move very quickly for his size and also be very strong? Or maybe you see a shorter man who's really fast, and can zigzag back and forth through small spaces? If you saw any of these—or someone in between—they are all correct.

Look at the players on a football team:

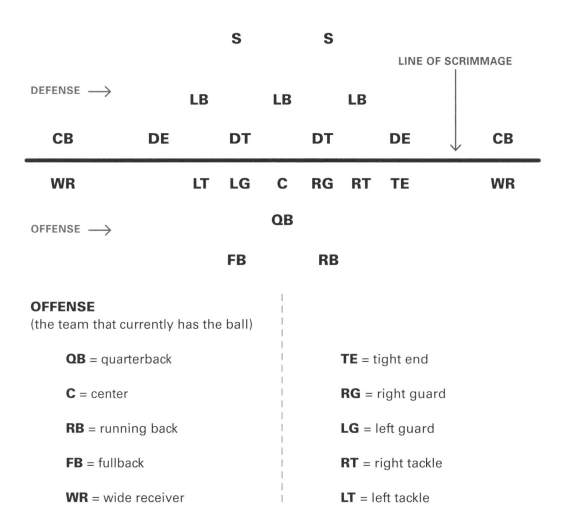

OFFENSE
(the team that currently has the ball)

QB = quarterback

C = center

RB = running back

FB = fullback

WR = wide receiver

TE = tight end

RG = right guard

LG = left guard

RT = right tackle

LT = left tackle

DEFENSE
(the team that does not currently have the ball)

DT = defensive tackle

DE = defensive end

LB = linebacker

S = safety

CB = cornerback

It makes sense that the biggest football players on the field tend to be the ones who are located on the line. This line is called the line of scrimmage, and that is where the ball is placed on the field based on its movement by the offensive team. These big players line up across from each other, and each team tries to keep the other from moving the ball. The players use their big muscles to push each other out of the way or away from the quarterback. On the offensive team, that means the center, the guards, and the tackles. On the defensive side, it's the defensive tackle and the defensive ends.

The other players tend to be smaller than the linemen, but much faster. These include the tight ends, fullbacks, and running backs on the offensive side. They must be strong to block players but also fast enough to run down the field and catch the ball if needed. Wide receivers are typically the fastest members of the offensive team, since they are the ones who will run down the field and catch the ball once it's thrown by the quarterback. They are covered by the cornerbacks and safeties on the defensive side who try to tackle them. As you can see, football players need to be in many shapes and sizes, but the two things all of them have in common are strength and speed.

Other sports where a large size can be an advantage include wrestling (as long as you stay within your required weight category), rugby, powerlifting, throwing shotput or hammer, and rowing.

Being smaller in size is helpful in many sports, too. As mentioned before, gymnastics is so much easier for shorter people. They can tuck themselves up very tightly and vault into the air, completing many rotations before they touch the ground. Smaller size is also great for running and cross-country, for biking, and even for competitive horseback riding. Being able to make yourself more compact on top of a horse will help reduce drag. If you're lighter, then the horse has less weight to carry.

Size does help in sports. But is there anything you can do about your size? Sure. You can lift weights to build up muscle. You can use nutrition wisely to help you put on lean muscle mass. But whatever you do, make sure you're doing it in a healthy way. Being fit is the ultimate goal!

HEIGHT HELPS

Height is also a big deal in sports. Being taller can really be useful for certain sports. Probably the first one most people think of is basketball. For either men's or women's basketball, being tall is an advantage. On the basketball court, the hoop is ten feet (3.05 meters) off the ground. The taller you are, the closer you are to the hoop, which means the chances of your getting the ball into the hoop are much higher.

The average height of most professional players that play in the National Basketball Association (NBA) is about six feet seven inches (about two meters). (That's about the same height as a camel.)

Of course, there have been some amazing basketball players that were much shorter. Here are just a few:

TYRONE "MUGGSY" BOGUES—5'3"

EARL BOYKINS—5'5"

MELVIN HIRSCH—5'6"

ANTHONY "SPUD" WEBB—5'7"

GREG GRANT—5'7"

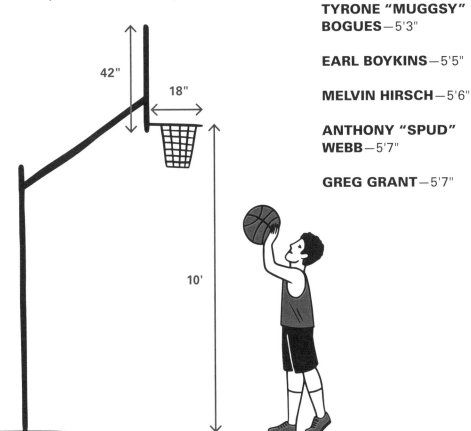

The average height for women in the Women's National Basketball Association (WNBA) is around six feet (1.83 meters). But there have been women as tall as seven feet, two inches in the sport.

Here are a few WNBA players:

MARGO DYDEK—7'2"

MARIA STEPANOVA—6'8"

LINDSAY TAYLOR—6'8"

ZHENG HAIXIA—6'8"

LIZ CAMBAGE—6'8"

BRITTANY GRINER—6'8"

According to many coaches, though, being tall isn't the only thing that can make a great basketball player. You need speed, endurance, versatility (meaning you can start, stop, and change direction easily), and yes, you need to be able to jump high! (Not high-jump—that's a different sport.) So don't worry if you aren't that tall—you can still play basketball well.

IT'S ALL ABOUT THE HANDS

TALL PEOPLE NOT only have height, but they also have large hands and feet. A larger than normal hand is extremely helpful in basketball. Why? If your hand is so big that it can span the entire basketball, then you can do what is called palming the basketball.

(text continues on page 22)

Your long fingers will be able to grip the basketball much more tightly than someone with a smaller hand. This means you'll be able to control the ball well, maneuver it without losing control, and grip it more tightly to aim and shoot accurately. Huge hands, like those of 6-time NBA champion Michael Jordan, are a great advantage in basketball!

Another sport with tall athletes is swimming. That may seem a bit strange, because they lie down while they compete. But when you are tall, you also have a long wingspan. In this case, wingspan doesn't just apply to a bird, it makes a difference to a human being, too.

Michael Phelps holds 28 Olympic medals and is one of the greatest swimmers ever; he is 6'4" (1.93 m) and has a wingspan of 6'7" (2.04 m). Missy Franklin, a 6-time Olympic medalist, is 6'2" (1.88 m) and has a wingspan of 6'4" (1.93 m).

Both of them have wingspans that are 2 inches longer than their height. Kind of seems like wingspan might be a very important trait for swimmers to have, doesn't it? Wonder what your wingspan is? Measure it.

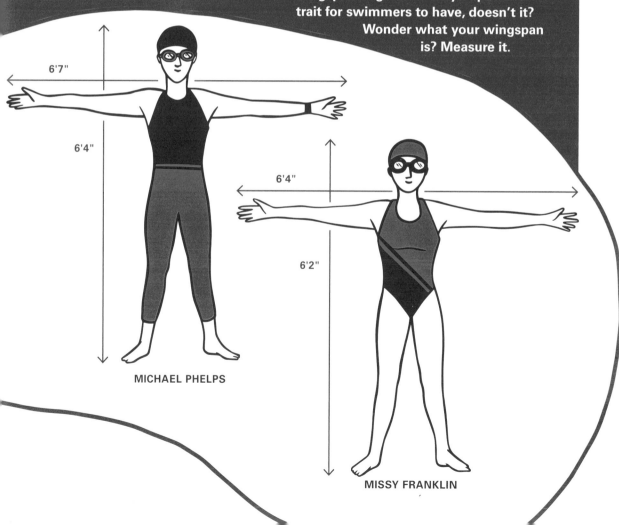

MICHAEL PHELPS

MISSY FRANKLIN

MEASURING YOUR WINGSPAN

HERE'S WHAT YOU'LL NEED:

- A measuring tape
- A friend

STAND UP STRAIGHT. Hold both arms out at shoulder height. Have your friend measure from the tip of your middle finger on one hand to the tip of your middle finger on the other hand. Now have them measure your height—from the top of your head to the ground. Compare the two. Your wingspan can sometimes be roughly equal to your height, or at least close.

Why is wingspan such a great thing in swimming? The longer your arms are, the farther you can stretch them out. And, more importantly, the more water you can pull and put behind you with each stroke. This propels you farther than, say, someone who might be a little shorter. A long wingspan is also great for that photo finish when the tip of your finger is needed to out-touch your competitor.

Other sports where a little extra wingspan could prove helpful are volleyball, tennis, and football.

There is nothing that you can do to make your wingspan longer. It depends on how tall you grow. Remember this: Just because your wingspan is not that wide doesn't mean you cannot be a great basketball player or swimmer. If that is your goal, go for it!

MEASURING YOUR VERTICAL LEAP

HERE'S WHAT YOU'LL NEED:

- A chair
- A friend
- A measuring tape

WHEN YOU THINK of a sport that needs someone to jump high, your first thought may be basketball. Basketball, of course, needs people who can jump high. That jump is called a vertical leap. This term means how high you can jump from a standing position straight up into the air. Wonder how high you can jump?

Grab a chair, a friend, and some measuring tape. The chair can be of any height. It's just there to give your friend some perspective as they watch you jump. Since the chair doesn't move, when you jump, your friend can note how high you jump compared to the chair. Then they can use the measuring tape to measure from that point to the floor. That tells you the height of your vertical leap.

Are you ready? Bend your knees. Swing your arms back (if you want) and jump straight up as high as you can!

Have your friend note on the height of the chair how high your feet went. Then have them measure that with the measuring tape. Switch places and have your friend jump. Then compare heights. Did one of you swing your arms more? Get a running start? Explore different ways you can get your jump higher.

What other sports involve jumping really high?

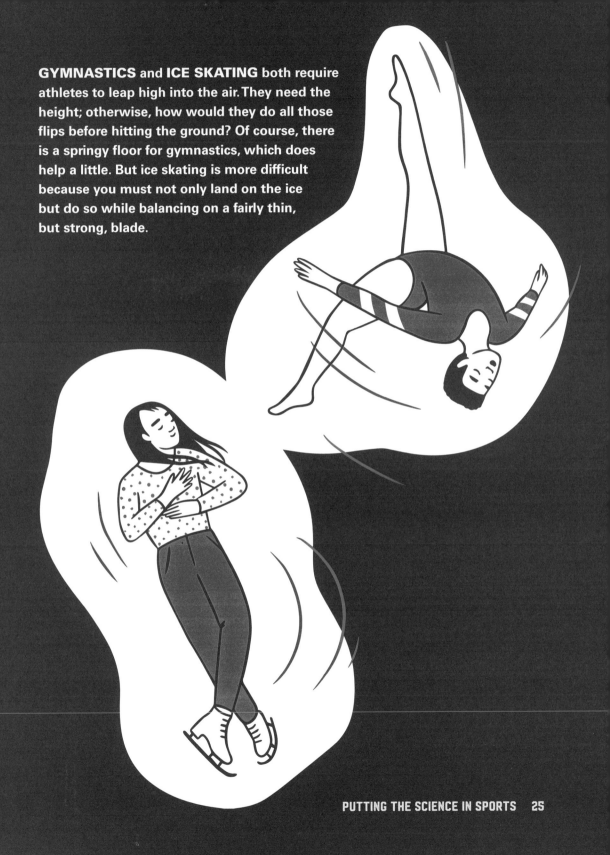

GYMNASTICS and **ICE SKATING** both require athletes to leap high into the air. They need the height; otherwise, how would they do all those flips before hitting the ground? Of course, there is a springy floor for gymnastics, which does help a little. But ice skating is more difficult because you must not only land on the ice but do so while balancing on a fairly thin, but strong, blade.

In **TRACK**, athletes need to be great jumpers for both the long jump and the high jump.

For the **LONG JUMP**, it's more of a forward leap as you are trying to cover as much ground horizontally as you can.

HIGH JUMP does require a vertical leap, but it's done backward. It also adds a bit of a flip of your feet at the end. (The jump doesn't count if the bar doesn't stay up.)

SOCCER players sometimes must jump high to block a ball or to kick it into the goal.

Can you work on your vertical leap? Sure. The power for a good vertical leap comes from your legs. So if you build up the muscles in your legs, you may be able to increase your vertical leap. A few things you can do are:

LUNGE

CLIMB STAIRS

It can take a while for your vertical leap to improve. As you have probably heard from your coach or trainer, or maybe your parents, *practice, practice, practice*.

SQUAT

PRACTICE JUMPING

FLEXIBILITY MATTERS

An athlete needs to be able to move quickly, to dodge, turn, jump, dive, and run. It is important that their body is ready to do all these things. Flexibility, or the ability to move your joints and muscles in a complete range of motion, helps with that. Wait. What is range of motion? *Range of motion* describes the movement that you can make at one of your joints. For example, most people can make a circle with their arm from the shoulder (a joint). They can also make a circle with their forearm at the elbow joint. Rotating your foot at the ankle joint and rotating your leg at your hip and knee are also examples of flexibility.

Flexibility in sports is important for a couple of reasons. First, it helps to prevent injury. Have you ever seen an athlete doing stretches before their performance? Hopefully that answer is yes. Most athletes do stretches, jog in place, and sometimes do little exercises before their event. This helps their muscles to warm up. In fact, the coach probably even calls it a warm-up. Basically, what happens is your muscles move around, get the blood flowing and your heart pumping a little. The stretching helps to loosen up any muscles that may be tight. A tight muscle does not respond as quickly as a loose one. Doing an activity with tight muscles can cause strains or other injuries.

Being flexible also means being limber, which means that you can move easily. Having loose, limber muscles is good for athletes. Muscles that are warmed up will be able to move rapidly and strongly as they are needed.

HOW FAST DO YOU REACT?

So far you've learned about height, wingspan, jumping, flexibility, and size. What's left? Speed and agility are two things that are really important in most sports. They are not the same thing, though.

Speed is how fast you can move. For many sports, like lacrosse, soccer, football, basketball, and running, just to name a few, that means how fast you can run. Of course, speed can also refer to how fast you can swim, or skate. Since most sports have some sort of time factor, you need to get across the finish line, complete the pass, score the goal, or even finish your performance in the time that is allowed. That means you need to be speedy!

LOOSEN UP!

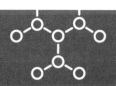

STAND TALL WITH your legs bent just a tiny bit at the knees. Bend at the waist and try to touch your fingers to the tops of your feet. Did you make it? If you did, you are pretty flexible. Can you put the palm of your hand on the ground next to your feet? Don't push this if you can't! But if you are able to get your palm on the ground, then you are very flexible.

Want to work on your flexibility? Practice doing stretches like this every day. Don't push yourself farther than you can go. But the more often you stretch, the more likely your flexibility will increase.

Agility refers to how easily you can move. Can you start, stop, switch directions, do flips, move from side to side quickly? That is very important for many sports. Particularly ones like lacrosse, soccer, football, basketball, tennis, and many others.

Take a look at this soccer field:

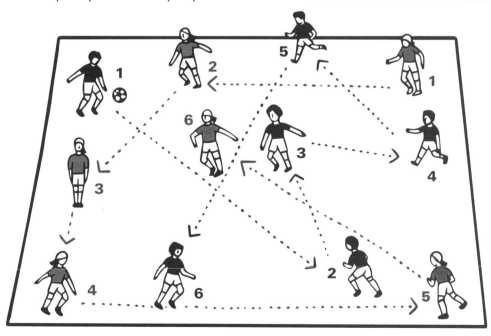

Check out the planned movement of these two figures on the field. The one player starts at #1 and moves to the #6 position. The other player follows its own path from #1 to #6. Notice they are both moving back and forth, forward, sideways, diagonally, and so on. This is naturally done while running pretty close to top speed. As a player you are expected to do all of this plus stop, turn, dodge, and kick as needed to either move the ball across the field (offense) or prevent it from being moved (defense).

In professional soccer, the players can stay on the field for two 45-minute halves, with only a short fifteen-minute break at halftime. That's basically ninety minutes of running around at top speed, and constantly stopping and maneuvering to win. Whew! Are you tired yet?

This same sort of fast and agile play is expected in many other sports. Here is a women's lacrosse play diagram (below). There are seven players on each side and two goalies. This is a drill for them to practice running and tossing the ball to each other. The player at the end shoots the ball into the goal. Looks confusing, doesn't it? And yet if it is executed properly, the players seem to flow as a team while moving the ball across the field…and score!

Being able to move, turn, and dodge while running at top speed and carrying a ball in your lacrosse stick is not easy. Think you can do it? Give it a shot.

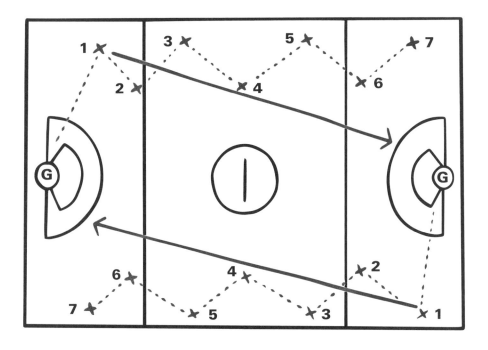

PRACTICE PASSING

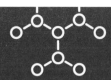

USE A LACROSSE stick to do this, or if you don't have one, improvise. Get an egg and a tablespoon. Place the egg in the tablespoon and hold the spoon out at arm's length. Now run around your backyard. Make sure you dodge, weave, and stop suddenly. Did the egg stay in the spoon? Good! You might make a great lacrosse player. If the egg went splat, don't worry. Just try it again. It takes a lot of practice to do all those movements while balancing a ball in a tiny mesh pocket in the lacrosse stick.

Is there anything you can do to your body to increase your speed and agility? Yes, somewhat. Part of your speed and agility is what you are born with, but you can do some exercises to improve on them if you want.

Here are a few ideas:

- Do short sprints
- Jump tiny hurdles
- Practice zigzag patterns—sprinting forward, stopping, turning and sprinting in a different direction
- Run with high knees

All of these will help you to build up the muscles in your legs, which should help with your speed and agility.

HOW FLEXIBLE ARE YOU?

THE LAST PART of agility is flexibility. As you probably guessed, gymnasts and ice skaters must be very flexible. What does that mean? Gymnasts should be able to tuck tightly into a ball so they can do all those somersaults in the air. Skaters bend their arms and legs in specific ways as they fly through the air or spin around and around. Actually, flexibility is really important in pretty much every sport. Being flexible makes things a lot easier on your muscles and joints. Stretching daily helps with that.

Time to test your flexibility with the butterfly stretch! Sit tall on the floor with the soles of your feet together and your knees bent out to your sides. Hold onto your ankles or feet, engage your abs, and slowly lower your body toward your feet as far as you can while pressing your knees toward the floor. If you're too tight to bend over, simply press your knees down. Hold this stretch for anywhere from 30 seconds to 2 minutes.

BRAIN SCIENCE

Working out to get your body in shape for sports is very important. You want to be in the best possible physical shape when you are competing. That means lifting weights, doing sprint drills, working on jumping higher...but also giving your brain a workout. What? Your brain needs to be in shape, too? It's true! How you *think* while you're participating in a sport is a huge part of your performance. Do you play on a team? Then you need to think about how well you work with others. Is your sport an individual one? Then you need to be able to solve any problems you may encounter by yourself. Mental fitness is just as important as physical fitness in sports.

Have you heard of the saying, "Practice makes perfect"? Well, practice may not make you *perfect*, but it will help you improve at your sport. It must; otherwise, why would so many athletes spend hours and hours a day practicing? Much of that practice time will be spent running drills,

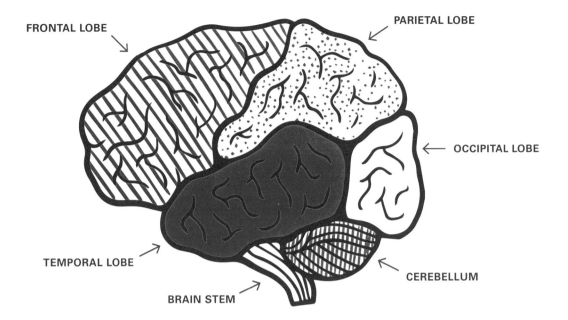

FRONTAL LOBE

PARIETAL LOBE

OCCIPITAL LOBE

TEMPORAL LOBE

CEREBELLUM

BRAIN STEM

or doing the same physical activity over and over. If you are a runner, you will run. If you are a swimmer, you will swim tons of laps. If you are a football, soccer, rugby, or lacrosse player, you'll spend many hours running, throwing, catching, kicking, and (hopefully) making goals. You may be surprised to learn that while you are doing all of these things with your body, your brain is working, too.

Your brain is a pretty cool organ. It's what runs all your body systems and, well, it keeps you alive. It is also the place where you process information. So learning how to use your brain in sports is very important.

What does your brain look like? Let's break it down into parts.

The *frontal lobe* is where you do most of your "big" thinking. It's

where you plan, organize, reason, and make changes to your behavior based on your environment. "Should I kick the ball to my teammate or take the shot myself?" The frontal lobe is where you make that decision. This lobe controls movement, too. Need to jump high to catch that football? This part of your brain will tell you to do it.

The *parietal lobe* helps you recognize and understand senses such as taste, touch, and smell. This is also where you calculate spatial relationships, like shapes, sizes, and distance. This part of your brain is really important for sports where you need to determine the distance to a ball or how far away you are from another player.

The *temporal lobe* is where you process sound. This is where you learn to tell the difference between the voice of your coach cheering you on and the whistle that stops the play. The temporal lobe is also where you store your memories. All that practice you are doing? All those plays you memorized? They are housed here.

The *occipital lobe* processes everything you see with your eyes.

The *cerebellum* controls balance and fine motor control, like how well you walk. You want to pay attention to this area, too. It will keep you from falling over—well, unless someone bumps into you. (Although your occipital lobe will hopefully give you a warning before that happens.)

Now that you know the parts of your brain, let's talk about how you can use it to help you in your sport.

FIND YOUR FOCUS

Whether you play a team or an individual sport, it is important to be focused on what you are doing. But since the focus is different for each of these, let's start first with an individual sport. What does your brain need to do when you're competing in an individual sport?

Individual sports like swimming, golf, and running require you to compete by yourself. It's just you against your competitor. You don't have anyone else to spur you on, or to help you catch up if you fall behind. It's all on you. That can be really exciting for some people and really scary for others. It also means that you need to focus on what you're doing. Sometimes your worst enemy is your own brain. It can make you doubt yourself. Or tell you that you don't have what it takes to win. While that isn't true, these internal thoughts can be tough for athletes to handle.

WHAT IS FOCUS?

Focus is the ability to direct your attention to one specific thing. It may be staring at something or maybe just intently watching one play. When you focus, sights and sounds going on around you seem to fade into the background.

Here's an example: A golfer prepares to putt the ball into the hole. He checks the angles of the putt. He looks at the grass to see if it's bumpy or level. He sets up his club at just the right spot. He is working out the exact place to putt the ball. While he is performing these tasks, he must ignore the hundreds of people standing around watching him. He concentrates, perhaps imagining hitting the ball in just the right spot. Then he putts. Hopefully, he hits it into the cup.

While the pro golfers on television make it look simple, performing in front of a huge crowd is anything but easy. Distractions are everywhere—with people moving about, talking, sitting, and maybe even making comments about your play. Practice helps the golfer to tune out those sounds and concentrate on their own moves so they can play their best game.

Of course, golfers are just one example of individual athletes who must have laser-sharp focus. The list also includes tennis players, swimmers, bowlers, and so many more.

Tennis players balance on the balls of their feet as they stare silently across the court. They must be ready to respond when the ball comes flying across the net. Will they need to go left, dive right, run forward or backward? They must anticipate where they need to be in order to return the ball across the net quickly. If the other player leans back on their heels, the ball may fly faster. If their opponent leans to the right and swings, the ball may go hard left. Practice helps to keep a tennis player focused as their frontal lobe calculates where the ball will go. That focus means they have to ignore the people in the stands and any sounds that are around the tennis court. To allow themselves to hear outside sounds will only distract them from playing their best game.

How do athletes find this laser-type focus? They must train to tune out the sights and sounds around them.

That happens through many, many hours of practice. Remember that the temporal part of your brain is where memories are stored. Well, if you practice over and over and over, those memories become very strong. Your brain learns what it must do to succeed in your sport. And it does it almost without thinking. Of course, that isn't literally true because your brain is always thinking. But it does mean that your brain becomes so used to doing these same motions over and over that it doesn't really need to tell your muscles what do to. They just do it naturally.

Why do you think athletes spend four to six hours (or more) practicing every day? They are memorizing the moves of their routines or their plays by doing the same thing over and over. That's why you practice: to train your brain to do an activity without really having to think about it.

HOW TO FOCUS

Do you play a sport? How do you maintain your focus? Here are a few things that may help:

- When you are playing, be in the moment. That means think only about the play in front of you. Or the part of the routine you are doing at that time. Don't think ahead. This can mess you up.

- If you find your thoughts moving ahead or you start thinking about something that is not a part of the game, stop. Give yourself a sort of mental shake, and then think about what you are doing right now.

- If you're nervous, take a deep breath. Sometimes just stopping for a second and taking a deep breath can calm you down. It also helps you regain your focus.

- Imagine the action you are going to do before you do it. Tap into your temporal lobe and your memories. You have done this action—i.e., putting the golf ball, swimming laps, hitting the tennis ball across the net—probably thousands of times. Just close your eyes and see yourself doing it correctly. That can focus your brain and help you to succeed.

TEAM SPORTS AND FOCUS

Being on a team requires focus, too, but it's a slightly different kind of focus. Team play requires you to be aware of everyone on your team who is in the game. You need to know your position on the field. Are you supposed to play in a certain area of the field? Maybe you're supposed to defend the goal or shoot the ball into the net from a particular angle? Take a look at the positions you might be playing in a soccer game (see illustration on next page).

For the most part, when you are assigned a position, that's the part of the field you play. Your job is either to attack—which means to advance the ball down the field toward the goal—or to defend, which means to keep the other team from getting the ball past you to score a goal.

This is not always an easy task. That is why you must work together with your teammates to accomplish it. You need to be aware of where you are on the field, where your teammates are, and also the position of the players on the other team. That is a lot to juggle at once. Here is where your focus is needed. You can do a much better job of keeping track of everyone and the ball if you really concentrate on what you are doing at that moment. What you need to be doing is thinking about where your teammates play and where they may move on the field. If you get good

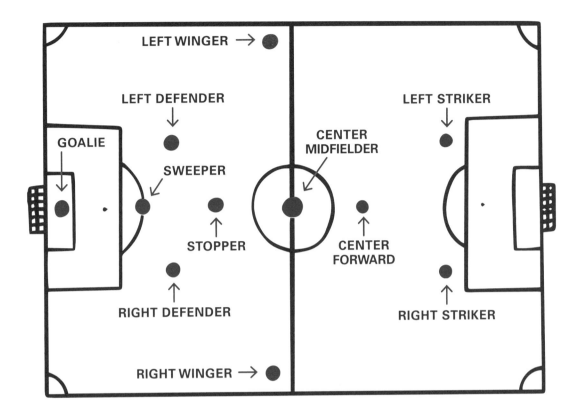

LEFT WINGER →

LEFT DEFENDER ↓

GOALIE ↓

SWEEPER

CENTER MIDFIELDER ↓

LEFT STRIKER ↓

STOPPER ↑

CENTER FORWARD ↑

RIGHT DEFENDER ↑

RIGHT STRIKER ↑

RIGHT WINGER →

enough at this, you can start to anticipate where your teammates will move, so that you can kick the ball there ahead of them.

Good team players also understand when it's best for them to keep the ball and when they should pass to someone who might be able to take a good shot toward the goal.

Here's an example: You have the soccer ball in the middle of the field. You know you want to score, but there is a player in the way who is preventing you from moving to the goal. You need to pass the ball to someone else. You look up, look around, and suddenly spot your teammate. Right where she is supposed to be. You kick the ball toward her, then quickly follow up to help defend her shot. GOAL! What were you focusing on?

1. The ball you have at your feet

2. Then finding your teammate

3. Then kicking the ball to a place where your teammate can reach it

PRACTICE YOUR FOCUS

GO TO YOUR room, where it's quiet. But take your phone or whatever you use to listen to music. Stand in your room and close your eyes. While it's quiet, go through the steps of something you do in your sport. For example, if you're a swimmer, imagine the feel of the cool water against your skin. Think of how it feels to take a stroke, pushing the water behind you and propelling yourself forward. Keep seeing this in your brain as you imagine swimming an entire lap. That is called mental imagery. And it is a very powerful way to hone your focus.

Now try it again. But this time turn on your music, very loudly. Maybe turn on a song that you really like and know the words to. Go back to your mental imagery. Can you easily slip back into the feeling of swimming? Or is it tough to focus with the song playing in your head?

If you find that your brain starts singing the song, stop. Take a deep breath. Concentrate and try again. Keep working on this until the song fades to the background and all you can see is you swimming along in the pool.

Of course, you don't have to use swimming for your mental image. Choose whatever sport you participate in. Practicing this over and over will help you to block out the sights and sounds that might distract you when you are competing.

If you were thinking about something else, say, what you were going to have for dinner, you would not be focused on the game. And the defender might have taken the ball from you and scored. How did you know that your teammate would be there? Practice. Coaches run drills over and over again to help players learn where they should be during the actual game.

LOSING FOCUS DURING PRACTICE

WHAT HAPPENS IF you lose focus in practice? Let's face it, sometimes practice can be boring. If your practice is swimming a ton of laps for hours a day or maybe running miles and miles, that can take a long time. You are swimming the laps so that your body can practice the strokes. But you are also doing it to stay in top physical shape. Same goes for running. If you find your mind wandering during practice, distract it. Maybe put your body on autopilot and allow your brain to wander. Give it a break. Sing songs in your head. Play back your favorite movie or book. Or maybe solve all of your math homework as you swim. It's a relaxing way to get things done while working out.

Of course, if your practice is catching a football, then you should stay focused. After all, if you aren't aware of your surroundings, *bam!* You could get tackled unexpectedly. Ouch!

So, because you have practiced with your team, you knew your teammate would be in that position at that specific time. You trusted her to be there and she was there. What a great play!

How do you stay focused during the game? Come on, you know this one—practice! Yep. Practice helps you focus. The best teams practice many drills daily so that working together becomes as easy as walking down the street. You don't even have to think about playing, because you know when you kick the ball to that side of the field your teammate will be there. That being said, you still need to focus on the game as it is happening. Because you also need to be where your teammate is expecting you!

Give these tips a try next time you are in a game or doing your routine. They can definitely come in handy.

Don't worry if they don't work the first time. Just practice them. (You knew that was the answer, right? Practice is *always* the answer.)

BALANCING ACT

Balance is controlled mostly by the cerebellum. Wonder where that is? Take your hand and put it at the base of your skull. Feel those two bumps on either side of your head? Those are part of your cerebellum. Your cerebellum needs input from two things in order to maintain your balance: your eyes and your ears.

Want to test your balance? Close your eyes. Now stand on one foot. Count to ten. Is it easy? Do you wobble back and forth, or are you steady as a rock? This gives you an indication of how good your balance is. Another way to test your balance is

to go outside and draw a line on the sidewalk with a piece of chalk. Stick your hands out straight from your shoulders. Then walk along the line, putting one foot directly in front of the other on the line. Can you walk the entire line without taking a step off? Good. You have great balance.

Why is balance important in sports? Well, for one, it keeps you from falling down. A good thing in most cases. But balance can be especially important for gymnasts. Particularly when they are on the balance beam? (Hint: If it's in the name, it's probably really important.)

A balance beam used in the Olympics is 16.4 feet (5 meters) long, 4 inches (10 centimeters) wide, and is 4.1 feet (125 centimeters) off the floor. This particular apparatus is very narrow, not easy to master, and is totally dependent on the gymnast balancing just right. Not only do they walk across it, they jump, leap, flip, and do back handsprings on this tiny platform. These gymnasts must really be in tune with their cerebellums!

Like to surf? You will need balance for that, too. Keep your feet apart, with one foot in front of the other, and stay low to the board. Once you get your balance, then you can stand up and ride the waves. Surf's Up!

Balance is needed for pretty much all sports. It's helpful in baseball, fencing, golf, boxing, and yes, even table tennis.

Is there a way you can improve your balance? Yep. Here are a few simple exercises you can try at home:

STAND IN PLACE

Pick a space in your house that is empty but located near a chair or counter that you can hold on to for support. Stand sideways so the object you're using for support is on either your left side or your right side. Put one hand on your support. Then pick a spot on the wall to stare at. It can be simply a speck, a picture, a light, whatever. Keep your eyes fixed on that spot. Now lift your right leg off the ground so that the top of your leg is parallel with the floor. Let go of your support. Hold your leg steady as you count slowly to ten. Put your leg down. Repeat with your other leg. Keep doing this until you can stand on each leg for a count of twenty or more.

FITNESS FUN

So now you know that practice is meant to help you focus, to find your balance, and to work on your reaction time. But really, one of the most important parts of practicing is staying fit. Being in great physical shape is something that athletes have to work at for many hours, many days, many months...and sometimes even years. Being in shape for your sport is not just about winning, it's about being safe, too. An athlete who is in good physical shape will (hopefully) have fewer injuries.

As you've probably learned in science class, Isaac Newton's Third Law of Motion states that:

FOR EVERY ACTION, THERE IS AN EQUAL AND OPPOSITE REACTION.

Think of it this way, every time you push on something it pushes back on you. This law is extremely important in sports. Contact sports—which are sports where people can collide, tackle, or bump each other—have a lot of pushing. Watch two hockey players fighting for the puck, as they elbow each other and nudge each other with their hips to try to get the puck away. Are they staying still on the ice? Probably not. They are moving. That movement on the ice can be due to the energy of them pushing each other around. If one player is more fit and stronger, he may be able to push the other player around more easily. So being fit helps with strength.

That is why athletes lift weights and train to build muscle: so they can make themselves stronger, and so that they can be the one who pushes harder or perhaps be the one who can't be pushed. Strong muscles will also be able to handle more pounding. When you run a lot, your body takes a lot of pounding. Your foot hits the ground, sending force into your foot, up your leg, knee, hip, and torso, and into your shoulder. It's Newton's Third Law again. For every force you apply into the ground, such as running, the opposite force goes back into you.

This type of pounding can eventually cause injury if you aren't in shape. That is another reason why people need to practice. You need to build up your body's ability to perform for long periods of time. Most athletes don't start their practice at full speed. They start out slow, doing stretches and warm-up exercises. They want to get their bodies ready for the time when they need to go at full speed.

But what happens if you do injure yourself by starting out too fast during practice or when you are playing in a game? You feel pain. Pain is something that can happen to any athlete, or any person for that matter.

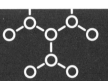

OUCH!

PAIN. It's part of an athlete's life. An athlete can experience pain at any time. Maybe they trip while running, pull a muscle, run into another player, or get hit by a ball. Those things hurt!

What do you do when you feel pain? Assess it, first. Is it a sharp pain? One that really hurts? If so, stop playing. If you are injured, you need to let your coach know that you need to go off the field so that you can have your injury looked at as soon as possible.

Pain is felt at the site of the injury, but then a signal travels up your nervous system to your brain. The thalamus is the part of your brain that processes that signal and sends it to your frontal lobe. That's when you feel the pain. Ouch!

(text continues on page 47)

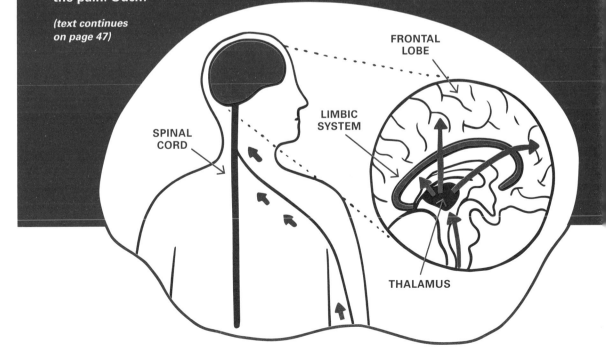

FRONTAL LOBE

LIMBIC SYSTEM

SPINAL CORD

THALAMUS

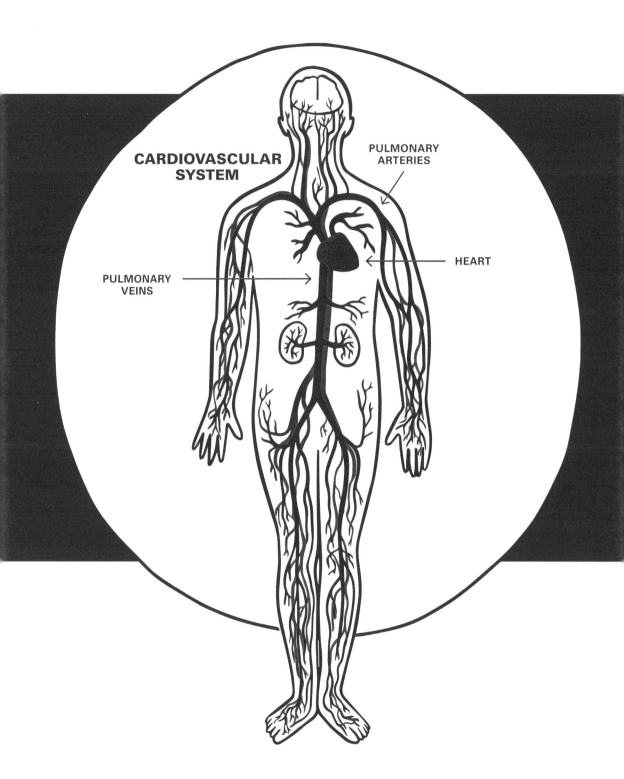

CARDIOVASCULAR
SYSTEM

PULMONARY
ARTERIES

HEART

PULMONARY
VEINS

You may have heard the saying, "No pain, no gain." Even though it's said a lot, it's not a great motto for an athlete. There are different kinds of pain. If it's sharp and hurts a lot, then it means you need to stop what you're doing right away. If it's a dull pain, then maybe you can keep playing but more carefully. If it's more of an ache in your muscle, then perhaps you just worked out too much the day before. In any of these cases, it's always best to acknowledge your own pain, and to tell your parents and coach about it. It is never a good idea to ignore pain. Pain is your body's way of saying that something might be wrong. Even if it's just an ache, pay attention. Perhaps you need to adjust your workout to make it less demanding, or maybe take a day of rest to recover.

Fitness also helps with endurance. Running a marathon takes a long time, and marathon runners have to be in great shape to be able to keep going for 26.2 miles. Not only do they run for 2–3 hours straight (no breaks), but they do it as fast as they can. To be that fit means that you have to have a great cardiovascular and respiratory system. Those are fancy words for heart, blood vessels, and lungs.

The cardiovascular system is made up of your heart and all of the blood vessels in your body.

Your heart is the organ that pumps blood throughout your body through the blood vessels. The blood vessels circulate blood and oxygen to every part of your body—your muscles, bones, lungs, and tissue (skin). Your muscles, bones, and skin need oxygen to survive.

FIND YOUR PULSE

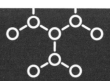

EVER FELT YOUR pulse? That's your heart rate. To determine your heart rate, count the number of pulses you feel in your vein as blood is moving through it.

Give it a try: Place your finger (not your thumb!) on the raised vein inside your wrist. Push lightly—not hard. Do you feel that thumping? That is your heart beating as it pumps blood through your body. If you count it for 10 seconds and multiply the total count by 6 you will get the beats per minute (bpm) of your pulse.

A normal resting heart rate, one that you take while you are sitting down, should be between 70 and 120 bpm for a 5- to 12-year-old child. The pulse rate of someone who is exercising can be much higher.

Why do we care about a person's pulse? It's normal to have a higher pulse when you are exercising. After all, you are working your arms and legs while you run, jump, or swim. That means your body needs more

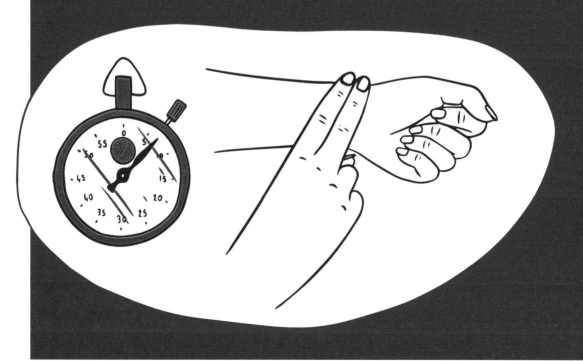

blood and more oxygen, and your heart has to pump faster to provide that. So of course your pulse goes up. That is normal, for the most part. The thing is, you never want your heart rate to get too high, or it can cause you to feel dizzy and perhaps pass out.

What's really interesting is that being in shape keeps your heart rate lower when you are resting. It's true. If you work out a lot your heart gets used to pumping at a higher rate, and it becomes more efficient. It figures out how to deliver the higher amount of oxygen you need while training, and then it can dip back down quickly into a lower resting heart rate.

The other important part about being fit is having a good respiratory system. The respiratory system is made up of your lungs, your airways, and your blood vessels, which get the oxygen they need here.

Your airway is made up of your nose, mouth, and trachea. When you breathe in, air flows into your airway and travels down the trachea to

(text continues on page 50)

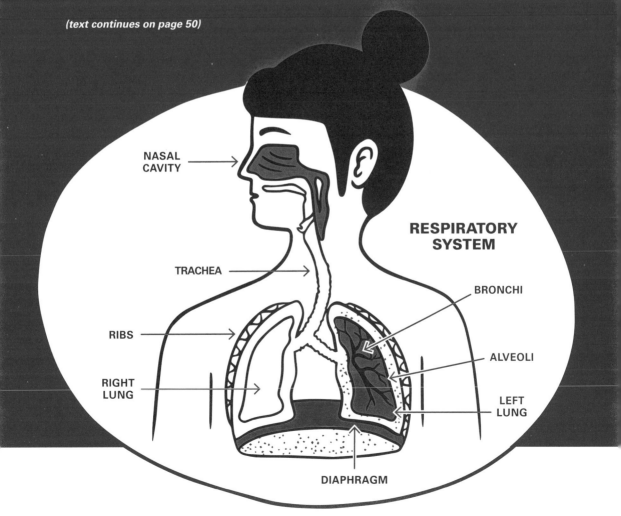

RESPIRATORY SYSTEM

NASAL CAVITY

TRACHEA

BRONCHI

RIBS

ALVEOLI

RIGHT LUNG

LEFT LUNG

DIAPHRAGM

your lungs. The bronchi send the air into your lungs where the oxygen is removed from the air. The rest of the air is expelled from the lungs and goes out the same way it came in (it is exhaled).

In the lungs the oxygen is absorbed by the blood and taken to the heart for pumping to your muscles. So you can see that the heart, lungs, and blood vessels all work together to keep you alive and fit.

When you practice, you exercise your heart, lungs, and muscles. They work together to pump your blood faster, providing you with more oxygen to keep you moving quickly. Staying in shape is better for your body and helps you to increase your endurance.

Someone who doesn't exercise a lot is going to find it much more difficult to finish a marathon than someone who practices running long distances every day. The marathoner who practices frequently is going to have a more efficient cardiovascular and respiratory system.

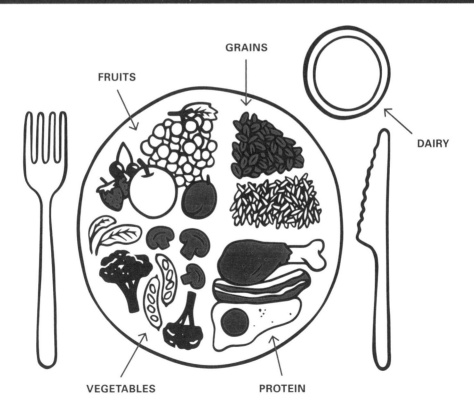

WHAT TYPE OF FITNESS IS NEEDED FOR EACH SPORT?

IF YOU ARE going to play any type of sport, you should have a certain level of fitness. For example, you should have a good cardiovascular system. That means you need to have a healthy heart and lungs so you'll be able to run, swim, jump, dive, etc. For sports like weight lifting, long jump, high jump, speed skating, cycling, and hockey you will also need really strong leg muscles. Having strong arms is similarly important for sports like baseball, volleyball, tennis, golf, football, and rugby.

But really, to be a good athlete your whole body needs to be in good shape. Your coach or trainer will help you focus on the areas that may need more strength than others. Being fit is a great way to do well at your sport, but it also helps you prevent injury. So actually, it's a win-win (and in sports, that is a great situation to be in!).

FILL 'ER UP

The last important aspect of body science is nutrition. Nutrition is the process of taking in food in order to fuel our bodies. Eating and drinking properly is important to every person, whether they're an athlete or not. Your body needs food and drink—and water specifically—to survive. Each type of food is processed in its own way so that it can provide you with energy. Some foods give you more energy than others. What is the best way to balance what you eat? Check out the cool food plate by the USDA on the bottom of page 50.

Each area of the plate contains a different type of food. Fruits and vegetables should make up about half your plate. One quarter of your plate should be made up of whole grains, (like breads and pasta) and healthy fats and oils. The last quarter of your plate is made up of proteins such as nuts, seeds, beans, fish, chicken, and eggs. Protein helps you build muscle, bones, skin, and hair. Then you have a separate area that is dairy. There you will find milk, cheese, yogurt, and more. You'll notice that the plate doesn't have a place for refined sugars—that's stuff like cakes and cookies. It is fine to eat this type of food, but do so only within limits. You don't want your plate to be overwhelmed because you are eating a ton of cookies and not many fruits and vegetables.

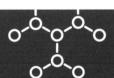

MAKE A FOOD JOURNAL

WANT TO FIGURE out what your food plate looks like? Keep a food journal. Write down everything you eat for 1–2 weeks in a notebook. Then go back and compare it to the plate. What do you see? Are you eating a lot of one type of food and a little of others? Make adjustments if possible to get a more standard-type food pyramid.

Athletes who exercise every day need to eat a lot of food. That is fine, as long as they try to stick to the foods that will help them stay healthy. Eating a bunch of cookies tastes great and gives you a surge of energy. But soon after that surge, you'll be more tired than ever. Energy from sugary foods doesn't last long. It's better to have a sandwich with whole-grain bread and a protein like chicken or ham to give you fuel. That will last longer and keep your energy level high.

WHAT IS CARBO-LOADING?

HAVE YOU EVER heard a professional athlete talk about carbo-loading before an event? It might seem like a strange term, but it's actually short for carbohydrate loading, and it is a real thing. Carbohydrates are your body's main source of energy. You get them from eating sugars and starches (milk, yogurt, beans, potatoes, and, yes, sweets). Your body digests these foods and turns them into energy for your muscles. That energy is stored as glycogen, which is a form of glucose (sugar) that is stored in your liver and your muscles.

The thing is, your muscles can store only a small amount of glycogen. Use it up, and then your muscles start to fatigue, or get tired. It takes about 90 minutes or less of intense exercise to use up all your glycogen. But if you are performing at a really high level, say biking or running for 3–5 hours, or even swimming that long, you can go through your glycogen stores faster.

Some athletes use carbo-loading to increase the amount of glycogen their body can store. How do you do that? About 3 days before your event, increase the amount of carbohydrates you are eating; maybe try eating a bunch of whole-grain pasta. At the same time, you should cut back a little on your workouts. This will prevent you from expending all of the energy you're storing in practice. Basically, you are trying to get your body to store as much energy as you can before your big game or performance. Does it work? Some athletes believe it does. Others may not really see a difference.

If you want to give it a try, be sure to ask your parents and/or your doctor first before getting started. It's better to be safe, and you also don't want to mess up your nutrition. Eating healthy is always a good plan, whether you are a professional athlete or not!

Don't forget to hydrate! That means drinking water or other fluids. Hydration is a very important part of staying fit. Your body needs water for all of its organs to work well. If you don't have enough fluids, your body will begin to get stressed. That means your organs have to work harder to keep pumping the blood around. If you are dehydrated, or are lacking water, you can get very sick. A dehydrated person might feel dizzy or nauseous, or even pass out. That is not a good thing. Doctors recommend that you drink up to eight glasses of water a day. That seems like a lot, so if you're small, maybe drink less. But if you're going to exercise a lot, particularly when it's hot outside, that may be the amount you need. Of course, you don't have to drink those glasses all at once. Space them out throughout the day.

To be well hydrated for your event, drink about 7–8 glasses of water the day before you plan to exercise or compete. About two to three hours before your event, drink at least a half or a whole bottle of water (about 16 ounces). While you are performing, you will want to keep drinking water, but only 2–3 gulps every twenty minutes or so. You don't want to drink too much, because that can also make you feel sick.

Be aware of how you're feeling while you are competing or exercising, too. If you are thirsty, try to stop for a drink. You don't need to drink a whole cup of water or fitness drink; just a few sips will help. Keeping hydrated during your sport will help you perform better, too.

Being an athlete means being aware of many different parts of science—biology, physics, and even life science. It may sound weird, but combining science and sports actually makes you a more informed and well-trained athlete. Now let's see how technology helps you perform better.

CHAPTER 2

THE *T* IN *SPORTS* STANDS FOR "TECHNOLOGY"

NOW THAT YOU know how to get your body in shape by practicing (are you tired of that word yet?), it's time to learn about other ways science can help improve your game. That means talking about technology. Science and technology are very important, especially in sporting equipment. After all, pretty much all sports require some sort of equipment. Just take a look below. Does any of this look familiar?

These are a good start to the list of sporting equipment, but there's so much more. How about running shoes? Balance beams or parallel bars? Or even swimsuits and speed skating suits? All of these are types of equipment. And just like an athlete, this equipment needs to perform at its best. This is where technology comes in. Did you know that much of the equipment used by athletes today has been developed by engineers and scientists? It's true. Athletes want equipment that will help them reduce drag, increase their efficiency, and keep them safe. How do you create something that can do all of that?

It's not easy. But it does help if you know a little bit about nanotechnology. Nanotechnology is the science of the very small, you could even say the microscopic. *Nano-* means something that is 10^{-9} or one-billionth of a meter (yes, that's billion with a *b*). To give you an idea of just how small that is, take a look at the chart on the opposite page.

One single strand of human hair is between 80,000 and 100,000 nanometers. That is *really* small! Why do we care about something so small? Well, when you make something out of nanofibers (which are 100 times smaller than a human hair), it is *very* strong. Some of the strongest things in the world are made of carbon nanofibers and nanotubes.

What is carbon? It is an element that is found naturally on Earth. You are probably most familiar with carbon as a form of carbon dioxide (CO_2). That is one of the gases that is found in our atmosphere. Plants absorb carbon dioxide and humans exhale it. (There is a whole carbon cycle on Earth.) Carbon is found in plants, animals, the atmosphere, and even in people. Why is it important in sports?

Carbon is capable of forming long chains of many individual carbon atoms. These long chains are very strong and rigid, but also light. Carbon is stronger than steel but as light as plastic. When you take these long chains—or fibers, as they are called—and weave them together, you get amazing products that are perfect for many different applications, including sports equipment.

Carbon fibers and carbon nanotubes are used to create tennis rackets, golf clubs, golf balls, racing bicycles, skis, hockey sticks, archery arrows, and swimsuits. Almost every piece of equipment you can think of contains some type of technology to help improve the athletes' performance or to keep them safe. Shall we take a look at what technology has created?

NANO: 10^{-9} m

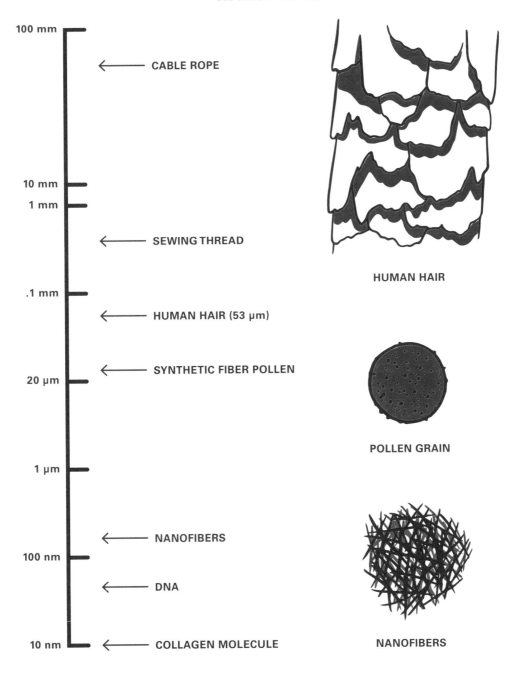

100 mm

← CABLE ROPE

10 mm
1 mm

← SEWING THREAD

HUMAN HAIR

.1 mm

← HUMAN HAIR (53 μm)

← SYNTHETIC FIBER POLLEN

20 μm

POLLEN GRAIN

1 μm

← NANOFIBERS

100 nm

← DNA

10 nm ← COLLAGEN MOLECULE

NANOFIBERS

WHAT IS A CARBON NANOTUBE?

CARBON NANOTUBES ARE made from flat sheets of carbon that are rolled up into a tube. Each sheet of carbon is bonded, or attached, to the others in an octagonal shape. It looks sort of like chicken wire you might see on a fence. But these tubes are definitely not as flimsy as a chicken wire fence. Carbon nanotubes are more than 400 times as strong as steel. Steel, as you know, is used to make buildings and bridges, so it's really heavy and strong. But carbon nanotubes are ⅙ the weight of a piece of steel that's the same size. Plus, they are very thin and can be molded into different structures.

How is this possible? Well, that is where chemistry comes in. The carbon nanotubes are made into a resin. A resin is a thick, sort of glue-like substance that hardens when its heated. Think of tree sap. It's liquid when it comes out of the tree, but hardens into a solid lump over time. The carbon nanotube resin is placed between the carbon fibers of a material and acts like a glue that holds everything together. That mixture of carbon fiber and nanotubes makes for a really strong material. Manufacturers use carbon nanotube resin for many different kinds of sports equipment.

SPEED AND POWER

As you know, speed is everything in sports. Many of them are timed, after all. The faster you run or swim, the more likely you are to win the race, and the same goes for bicycling and skating. Think of it this way: If you had a piece of equipment that could possibly make you go faster, wouldn't you use it? Sure. Why not? If it was legal in the sport—as most technology is—most people would jump at the chance.

That was what the people who produce bicycles thought, too. Being a professional cyclist is tough. Most likely you are riding up hills, or mountains even, and possibly racing along steep cliffs with no guardrails, and with a pack of people next to you. Sounds a bit scary. Add to that scenario the big piece of equipment you are using to propel yourself up that hill or mountain. Whew! Are you tired yet?

What if there was a way to give you a bike that was really strong but weighed a lot less? You'd take it, wouldn't you? That's good, because the cycling companies have been using nanotechnology for years to make bikes that are strong and lightweight.

Carbon nanotubes have allowed bike manufacturers to make racing bicycle frames that weigh less than 2.2 pounds (1 kilogram). That means an entire bike, including the wheels, can weigh less than fifteen pounds depending on the size of bike you choose. But that same bike will also be 20 percent stronger than previous bicycles, which means that it should hold up under more wear and tear. If a bike weighs less, then it will take less energy to make the bike move. So if you use the same amount of energy, you should (ideally) go farther and faster on this new, lighter bike. Does it work? Well, bikes made with this new technology have been used in the Tour de France—the biggest cycling event in the world—for years.

Carbon nanotube technology is not just used in bicycles, but also in

golf clubs, hockey sticks, kayaks, and arrows used for archery. This technology has made everything stronger and lighter, which is definitely an advantage in competition. Remember physics and Newton's Third Law? The more something weighs, the more energy is required to move it.

When you think of nanotechnology and sports equipment, you might not think of swimsuits. But swimsuits were some of the first pieces of equipment to get a technological upgrade. It's kind of funny when you

think about it, but a swimsuit is actually a piece of sports equipment. It is supposed to help you cut down on drag, which in turn helps you swim faster with less effort. Sounds like a winning combination to me.

That means the only way to improve the technology of the swimsuit must involve changing the fabric that's used to make it. Every fabric has a different way of interacting with water. Cotton swimsuits soak up water, which makes them heavy, and as we all know weight slows you down. Cotton suits should not be worn in competition, although they are fine for hanging out at the pool with your friends.

If your goal is to win a competition, you will want to have a swimsuit made out of nylon, polyester, or spandex (the stretchy material that feels sleek and smooth to the touch). All of these suits have one main thing in common: they are hydrophobic, which means they repel water.

As you swim, the water is not absorbed by your suit, and instead it simply slides past you. That is one way to reduce drag. A lightweight, hydrophobic suit is good for competition, but if you really want to be one of the top swimmers, you might want to consider a suit that contains carbon fibers. Many companies are weaving carbon fibers into their

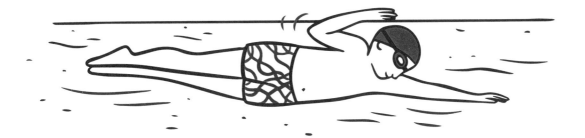

swimsuits to provide added strength and flexibility. The carbon fibers are sometimes wrapped around a strand of nylon and then woven in a crisscross pattern throughout the material. This makes the suit super-strong. It also gives the swimmer something more to help them with drag—compression.

Compression of the swimmer's body can also reduce drag. How does this work? Take a look at the body of a shark and compare it to a human.

A shark has a long, sleek body. The only parts that stick out from its body are the fins (on the top and the side), and its tail. But all those parts are shaped in such a way that they cut through the water quickly, without creating much drag at all. Sharks swim by moving their bodies from side to side. There is very little action to slow them down.

Now look at the human swimmer. While he appears to be long and lean, there are many places where his body can experience drag. His arms must be constantly moving. Every time they go out of the water and come back in, it slows him down. His body is also not exactly streamlined like the shark; there are different areas that might stick out, like his head and shoulders, which can increase drag.

If a human wears a compression suit, the suit does exactly what it advertises. It compresses the body into more of a streamlined shape.

See the difference in the illustration below.

Notice how their bodies appear to be tightly compressed and more stream-lined, like a shark's? This is a huge plus for reducing drag.

Now that swimsuits are made with carbon fibers, swimmers can have a more streamlined body for competitions. Does it help? Some people think so. The real question is whether or not you would think so if you were competing. Remember the part about brain science? A lot of how you compete is in your head. So if you think the compression suit helps, it probably does.

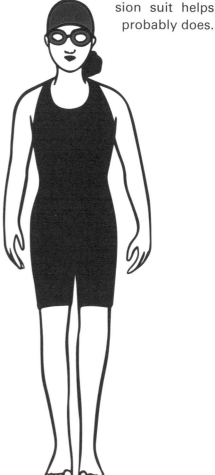

TESTING DRAG IN WATER

WANT TO SEE how drag affects you in water? Do this simple experiment. Fill your sink or bathtub about ⅓ full of fresh water.

HERE'S WHAT YOU'LL NEED:

- A ball (tennis, baseball, or whatever you have around)
- A spatula
- A pencil
- An empty juice box

Pick up 1 object and place it into the water. It should be at the end of the sink or tub.

Now, hold on to the object and push it through the water to the other side. Do you feel pressure pushing back on you? That is drag. Try each object separately. Assign each object a number for the amount of drag you feel, ranging from 1 to 5 (1 means very little drag; 5 means a lot of drag). What did you discover?

Most likely, the object that was the biggest and the least streamlined had the most drag. Now you know why compression suits are so helpful in swimming competitions.

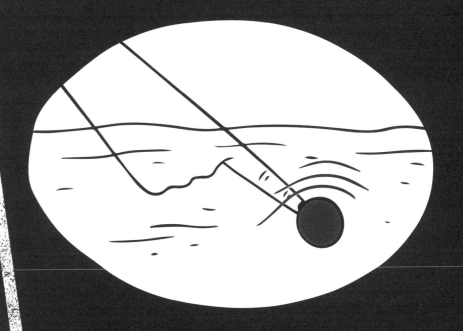

SAFETY FIRST!

Playing a contact sport, like football, lacrosse, or hockey, can be dangerous. Keeping an athlete safe should be the top priority of everyone on the field. That's why athletes in all these sports are required to wear helmets. The thing is, helmets can be uncomfortable. Have you ever worn one? If they are too big, they flop around on your head, and even come off. If they are too small, they feel tight and like they are pushing in on your brain. (They aren't, they just feel that way.) Having a helmet that fits snugly, but not too tightly, on your head is the best. Athletes also need to be sure that the chin strap—the thin piece of plastic that stretches across your chin from ear to ear—is snug, too. That will keep the helmet on and in place.

But what do you do if you are hit in the head really hard? Will that affect the level of the helmet's safety? It can. Plus, if you take a hard hit to the head, you definitely need to tell your coach. You need to be evaluated to make sure you don't have a concussion.

What is a concussion? A brain injury usually caused by a blow to the head. Or it could be a severe bump, a jolt, or some kind of abrupt, traumatic movement. The movement is so strong that it causes your brain to twist or bounce around inside your skull. This can damage the cells in your brain and is not good.

If you have a concussion, you may have a headache, feel nauseous (sick to your stomach), dizzy, or even see black spots in front of your eyes. You might appear dazed or stunned, and perhaps even pass out for a few seconds. If you have any of these symptoms, tell your coach and your parents immediately! Concussions can show up even a day or two after you've been hit in the head. You will probably have to see a doctor who will tell you what to do to take care of yourself. Most likely it will mean a lot of rest. Be sure to follow your doctor's orders and take your concussion seriously! You want to be back and up and around again soon.

Wouldn't it be great if there were helmets that could tell you—or your coach—just how bad a hit was? You could know right away if you needed to be worried that you were injured. Well, now you can.

Sensors have been created that can send information from an athlete's helmet to a device that a coach holds in their hand on the sideline. These small sensors are embedded inside the helmet and measure the impact that the athlete receives on their head. It tells the coach how hard the hit was, but also the direction and the location on the head where the player was hit. This type of information is invaluable to the coach and the player. It is a fast, efficient way of figuring out if a player has

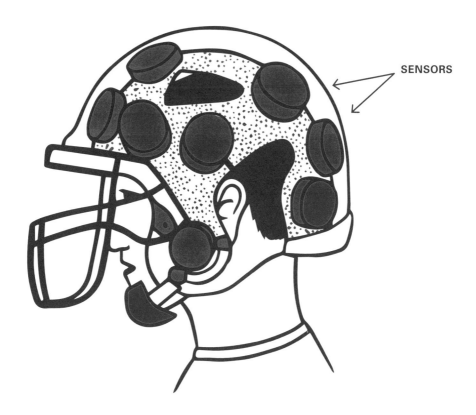

SENSORS

sustained a serious injury. If a player has been hit hard, the player will be removed right away and sent to the team doctor on site. Reacting to an injury fast is a great way to help keep athletes healthy.

HOW DO SENSORS WORK?

Sensors that can record movement are called inertial sensors. That is because they measure the inertia of your movement. They do that by recording the acceleration of your movement. In other words, every move that you make causes your body to have some sort of acceleration. If you are walking, your acceleration perhaps will be slow, but if you are running, your acceleration will be much faster. Accelerometers can also record how much of an impact your body receives (which is what they are used for in helmets). Any type of impact will cause a movement of your head. A stronger impact will increase acceleration and therefore cause your head to move a greater distance. It's this distance that the accelerometer is measuring.

A gyroscope is a sensor device that measures angular movement, or the distance an object moves at an angle from a fixed point. Wait. What? That is confusing. Think of it this way.

Straighten your arm and hold it out parallel to the ground. Now bend the lower part of your arm, below the elbow, to make it perpendicular to the ground (like in the image below).

A gyroscope would measure that movement as angular movement from your elbow. It is angular momentum because you changed the angle of your arm with respect to your elbow.

How does this work in a sensor? The gyroscope records a movement based on where it is placed on your body. If the sensor is on your head, then when your head moves, it will record the direction of the movement. For example, if you move your head to the right, the gyroscope will record that as an angular movement. But what happens if you get hit in the head? The gyroscope will record the movement of your head, and then you can tell from what direction you were hit.

Remember that if you are hit during a sport, your head will move in one direction. So then you can infer that the hit came from the opposite side. A hit that moves your head right came from your left. And a hit that moves your head left came from your right. Why do we care about this? With this information coaches can know exactly where the impact occurred on a player. That way they will know where the injury is and treat it properly.

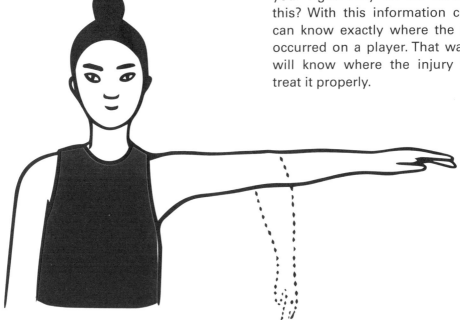

WHAT DOES AN IMPACT LOOK LIKE?

LET'S DO AN experiment. You will need a balloon. Blow up the balloon and tie it off. Hold the balloon in one hand.

Now punch the balloon with your other fist, just like it's a punching bag.

What happens to the balloon? It moves forward in the direction of the punch, and then back toward you. That is what any part of your body does when it feels an impact.

Now try punching the balloon with different levels of force. First hard, then soft, then medium. Notice that the balloon moves backward less after a lighter punch and more after a stronger one. If you had an accelerometer sensor attached to the balloon, you could measure all of these changes. It tells you how far your head moves when it gets hit. The farther your head moves, the harder the impact. Since greater impact can mean more chance of injury, this is important for coaches to know, don't you think?

Another place technology helps with safety is found in the player's mouth. It may sound strange, but mouthguards have sensors, and it's a good thing, too! Many different sports require mouthguards. They are a great way to protect your teeth. So if you have to wear one, why not wear a mouthguard that will also keep the rest of your body safe? These special mouthguards have a gyroscope, which tells the coach the exact position of their head when they were hit. It measures the amount and direction of the movement of the portion of the body that was struck. The mouthguards also send information to a device in the coach's hand. What great information to have in an instant!

A third type of sensor that measures impact to the head is a patch that's worn on the head itself. It has a sticky coating that allows the player to place it behind their ear. This patch is so small, it doesn't interfere with a helmet. It can also be worn during practice without helmets. The sensor gives all the same types of info—impact and direction of injury—and it also counts the number of times

the player has been hit in the head. Coaches are using this information to lessen the injuries sustained by their athletes.

STAYING SAFE ALSO MEANS STAYING HEALTHY

Staying safe doesn't just mean protection from hits and bumps. It also means staying healthy. Sickness is a sure way to interrupt your sports season. People become ill for many reasons, but bacteria and fungi are two things that can cause an infection. Bacteria are microscopic organisms that live pretty much everywhere in the world. In dirt and soil, in the

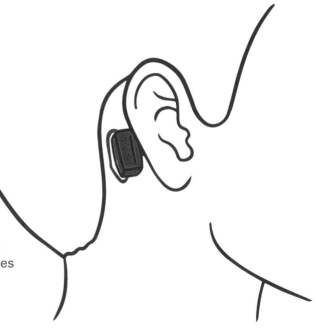

ocean, and even inside your body. That's right. You have bacteria that live in your intestines right now. Don't worry. They are there to help you digest your food. Bacteria are so small you can only see them under a microscope.

Humans have a strange relationship with bacteria. On the one hand, they are helpful to our digestion. On the other hand, bacteria can make us very sick. Illnesses caused by different bacteria include pneumonia, strep throat, food poisoning, and many more.

Fungi are also very small organisms, but they live mostly on land. Fungi are found in soil or on plant material. Yeast is a particular type of fungi that loves to live in warm, moist areas. While yeast is used to make bread and beer, it can also cause infections in humans.

Infections from bacteria usually require treatment by a doctor. In some cases, the doctor will put you on antibiotics, which are medicines that help you get well. While you have the infection, you might be tired, so you'll have to rest. Fungi can cause problems by giving you athlete's foot. You may have had it. Athlete's foot is when the skin on your feet and between your toes peels off. Your foot is very itchy—so itchy, in fact, that it drives you crazy.

What is the point of telling you all this? Technology can take care of it! That's right: Sports socks exist that can prevent athlete's foot. Companies are weaving tiny strands of silver nanoparticles into their socks. Silver is antibacterial and antifungal, which means it can prevent bacteria and fungi from growing. Silver nanoparticle fibers are not just used in socks, but also shorts, T-shirts, and, yes, even underwear. Guess what? It gets rid of the smell, too. No more smelly sports clothes.

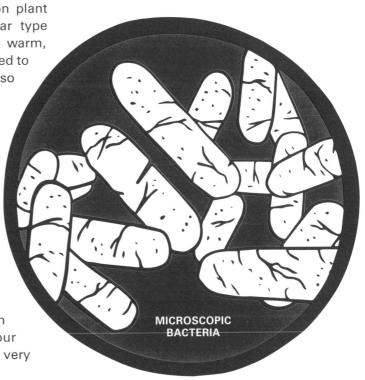

MICROSCOPIC
BACTERIA

WEARABLE TECHNOLOGY

What's this? It means exactly what it says. It is technology that you wear, and it is very popular with athletes. Actually, many people use wearable technology in their everyday lives. You may even have some on you right now. Do you have a watch that counts your steps? That is a pedometer. A pedometer is a less-fancy version of an accelerometer. The pedometer calculates the distance you have covered in one day by counting the distance of every step you take. An accelerometer gives you the distance and the speed that you are moving.

A device that helps you keep track of your health is called a fitness tracker. They are very popular in today's world. Fitness trackers can be worn on the wrist with a band, in a watch, or even as a clip-on to your belt. A fitness tracker can be a combination of many different things, depending on what type of information you want to gather.

It can be a pedometer or an accelerometer. One of these is typically included in every standard fitness tracker. Want to know how high you climbed in a day? You will need a GPS tracker on your watch. GPS, or Global Positioning System, uses satellites to track your movement. GPS is found in pretty much all cellular phones and in many fitness trackers.

A fitness tracker is also able to measure your pulse. Remember what that is? It is your heart rate—how fast your heart beats per minute. This is important if you're trying to reach a certain heart rate during your workout. A higher heart rate during exercise can indicate that you are getting a much more intense workout. If you exercise on a regular basis, it's good to know what your normal heart rate is, and when you've reached a high one. That way you will always work out safely. A heart rate that is too high during a workout can be dangerous. The fitness tracker will give you a number for your heart rate. Your heart rate during exercise should be less than two hundred beats per minute. If it's higher than that, let your parents and your doctor know so they can see if that is okay for you.

Some fitness trackers can even record your sleep patterns. A sleep tracker is made up of a combination of sensors. First, there is a heart rate monitor. When people are asleep their heart rate drops. This is normal. It happens because you are in a very relaxed state when you sleep. Another sensor measures your movement during sleep. This will tell you whether you are sleeping calmly, which means you're not doing a lot of moving around. Or if you are sleeping restlessly, which means you

are moving around a lot. Why does this matter? It is believed that calm sleep will help you to sleep better and feel more refreshed in the morning. Finally, some sleep trackers can measure your sleep stages.

There are two basic stages of sleep: REM, which stands for Rapid Eye Movement sleep, and non-REM sleep. REM sleep is deep sleep where you are dreaming. REM sleep is needed for you to feel rested in the morning. During the night, your brain flips from non-REM sleep to REM, and then back to non-REM. Each person has their own natural cycle of doing this. Your sleep cycle can be interrupted by sickness, stress, or even dreams that wake you up. By recording your sleep cycle with your fitness tracker, you may be able to learn something about when you sleep best and when you don't.

A fitness tracker can also record the amount of calories you've expended during the day. A calorie is a unit of energy. People need to eat a certain number of calories every day, and these calories come from food. The more food you eat, the more calories you take in. A child between the ages of six and twelve years old needs to eat between 1,600 and 2,200 calories every day.

TRACK YOUR DAILY CALORIES

WANT TO KNOW how many calories you are eating in a day? Keep a food journal. Different types of foods have more calories than others. For example, sugary treats tend to be higher in calories than vegetables. You can go online to the Choose My Plate website run by the USDA (U.S. Department of Agriculture). That will give you a journal and a list of the calorie amounts for many foods you might eat.

Can't find your food listed? Do an internet search for it. There are also apps you can get on your phone to help you track your calorie intake. It's always a great idea to see what you're eating to be sure you have a good, balanced diet.

Why so many? Just like a car needs fuel to run, so does your body. Except instead of gasoline, your body uses calories as its fuel. When you expend energy to move, you are burning calories. If you want to know how many calories you are using every day, get a fitness tracker. A fitness tracker uses your weight and keeps track of your exercise to calculate the number of calories you use. Weight plays a big part in calculating the number of calories you expend because it takes more energy to move a larger object. Just like a big semi truck uses more fuel to move than a small car.

The first thing you need to do when you get a fitness tracker is to enter your weight in pounds and sometimes your age. As you wear the tracker, it calculates how many calories you use to walk across the floor, up the stairs, or to jog two miles. Every person burns calories at a different rate. That rate is based on their metabolism, or how fast your body uses energy. That is where the age part comes in. Typically, the younger you are the faster the rate of your metabolism. Metabolism is also affected by your level of activity. If you're a professional athlete and you work out four to five hours a day, you will have a much higher metabolism than someone who does not work out as often.

Once you know how many calories you are burning in a normal day, you can compare that to how many calories you eat a day. If the amount of calories you burn is more than the calories you are eating, you may lose weight. If the amount of calories you burn is less than what you're eating, you may gain weight. The goal is to keep the two numbers fairly close to each other.

Don't have a fitness tracker? Use an app on your cellular phone. There are apps that can do the same thing a fitness tracker can do. But you have to keep your phone with you all the time. It can't track your steps if it's lying on your nightstand at home while you're at school.

That's why a lot of people have fitness trackers on their watches. Get up. Put on your watch, and forget it. Easy peasy.

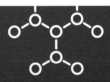

WHY DIDN'T MY BIKE RIDE COUNT?

EVER WORN A fitness tracker on your wrist and gone for a bike ride? Did it track your effort? Some fitness trackers that only have pedometers might not record a bike ride because you are not actually moving while you're on your bike. What? Think about it. As you ride your bike, your legs are moving, but your body is not. The same thing can happen with an accelerometer if it's on your wrist. If you want the movement of your feet counted as exercise, put the tracker on one of your legs or tie it to your shoe. It's sort of like outsmarting the tracker. But hey, you'll get to count your exercise for the day!

AIR BUBBLES

SENSE-IBLE SHOES

Another type of wearable technology is a running shoe. Maybe that's cheating to call it wearable technology. After all, you do *have* to wear a shoe. But it's true because running shoes these days are packed full of technology—from extra cushioning to added support, and even special sensors. Everything is designed to help the runner perform better and prevent injury.

Why is all this stuff needed? If you are a runner, you will understand. Runners experience a lot of different forces when they run, the greatest of which is impact. When your shoe hits the ground, the force of your body pounds into the ground. As we know from Newton's Third Law, for every action there is an equal and opposite reaction. That means as your foot pounds into the ground an equal amount of force is sent up through your foot and into the rest of your body. Your foot experiences two opposite forces at the same time. That's a lot of pressure. If you run barefoot, you will feel all of that force in your foot. Without cushioning or support your foot can start to hurt. That is why you wear running shoes.

Running shoes are different from regular shoes in that they help to cushion and support your foot as you run. The materials used to make a running shoe are designed to absorb the impact of your foot when it hits the ground. Over the past thirty years, cushioning in running shoes has greatly improved. In 1979, Nike began adding air to their shoes. They put small pouches of air into the midsoles—the middle of the shoe—to help cushion the foot. Imagine walking on a bunch of tiny balloons. As you step, the balloons are squished down but then pop back up when you lift your foot off the ground. Comfy, yes? It was. But there is always room for improvement.

In the mid-1980s ASICS decided that instead of air, a gel would cradle your foot in comfort. They added a gel support ring in the heel of their shoes and a separate ring of gel under the front of the foot. The squishy-soft gel was strong enough to support a runner's foot, but it also reduced impact.

Running shoes have changed a lot in the last thirty years. Technology has moved more toward making a shoe that can return some of your own energy back to you. Remember that for each step you take, some energy goes into the ground, but some energy also travels back up your leg. The idea is that if you can send more of the energy back to your leg, then it will be easier to run. Is that possible? No one knows for sure, but some shoe manufacturers make that claim. Think of it this way: If the shoes are bouncier, then some of the bounce will be absorbed by your legs. Runners who wear these cushion-enhanced shoes claim that the shoes make their legs feel more energized as they run.

The technology works by using a single piece of foam, which is created when shoemakers take hundreds of pea-sized bits of foam and steam them together using heat. These bits of foam are stuck together and used to make up the bottom of the shoe. If you assume there are tiny amounts of air between each of these bits of foam, that would make the shoe more flexible and provide greater bounce to the foot. Thus, the return of energy to the leg is greater. It's a bit like jogging on a surface that gives a little as you walk (not like a solid sidewalk or road, which doesn't give much at all).

Reebok went one step further when they added a new twist to air cushioning. Their shoes included an actual button that you pushed to pump the upper part of the shoe full of air. When you were wearing these shoes, your foot was quite literally encased in air. The idea was that the air could provide the best support for your foot and ankle. That was because it was pumped into the exact spaces that existed between your foot and the shoe. Did it work? Some people thought so. For a time, these shoes were quite popular, particularly with athletes whose sports required support for their ankles.

Want more support with your cushion? Shoe manufacturers have that covered as well. Nike makes a shoe that is cushiony but also provides support with a carbon fiber plate in its sole. The carbon fiber (yes, that is nanotechnology again) is placed between two pieces of foam to give the foam a little more support. This, in turn, supports your foot while cradling it in comfort. A great combination, especially if you run long distances like marathons.

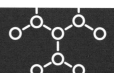

SAVE THE PLANET WITH YOUR SHOES

WANT SHOES THAT are eco-friendly? No problem. Brooks Running is one company that takes its dedication to the environment seriously. Their shoes are made from environmentally friendly materials. Many of them are made from recycled or sustainable products. A sustainable product is one that is created without using up nonrenewable resources, like oil or coal. Sustainable products are great for the environment because they have little to no impact on it. The best part is that most of the shoes made by Brooks Running will break down 50 times faster in a landfill than a regular running shoe. Go Green running!

PREVENTING INJURY

Technology is not just for helping you perform your best or keeping track of your fitness. It's also for preventing injury. The best way to prevent injury is to be in good physical shape, to always wear protective gear, and to play safely. But even with all of that, there is no guarantee that a player won't be injured during practice or a game. What if you play a sport where there isn't a lot of protective gear? Where the way you move your body is what can cause you injury? Two sports that don't have a lot of—or any—protective gear are baseball and golf. In both of these sports, you use a bat or a club to hit a ball. While it is possible to get hit in baseball—say when someone is preventing you from sliding into a base, or maybe if you collide with your teammate while catching a ball—most of your injuries will be self-inflicted. That's right. You can injure yourself just by your own movement. Sounds crazy doesn't it?

The cool thing is that technology can help with that. Golf and baseball come down to physics. It is the movement of your knees, hips, arms, body, and head that controls how hard you hit the ball. The faster and harder you hit the ball, the farther it will travel. You also want to be able to control the angle of the ball. A ball that is going higher will travel farther.

An athletic trainer can help you figure out the most efficient way to hit a ball, run a race, or shoot a basket. Athletic trainers are people who study a certain sport and then use their knowledge to help an athlete perform to the best of their abilities. Trainers also study an individual athlete by recording their biometric data. Biometric data is used to measure a person's physical characteristics, such as their heart rate, blood pressure, sleep patterns, fitness levels, and maybe even how much they sweat. By using biometric data, athletic trainers and coaches can see when the player has reached their maximum exercise capacity and then pull them out of practice. Another way to use biometrics is to film the athlete as they take their swings and record how they swing. By studying that film, the athlete, trainer, and coach can decide the best method to use when hitting a ball.

Think of it this way: If you are getting ready to hit a baseball, you go through several steps. First, you stand at home plate. You plant your feet, one in front of the other. You grip the bat with both hands, and pull it around and behind your head. Your eyes are focused on the pitcher's hand. When you see the pitcher release the ball, your muscles in your arms tense. You might lean

SHOULDER CLOSED
& RELAXED ARMS

EYES ON THE TARGET

KNEE & FOOT
TURNED
INWARD

WEIGHT AGAINST
THE BACK LEG

toward the pitcher, and finally you'll bring the bat forward and around fast. *Crack!* You hit the ball over the fence. At least that is what you hope will happen. But the action of moving the bat around has a lot of different effects on your body. By taking a video of the player swinging, a coach can analyze the manner of the swing. Is the player using all of their energy in the most efficient way? Are they swinging too hard and at the wrong angle? Are they having a hard time swinging a bat, which means they should switch to a lighter one? All of these suggestions can help a player to swing better and more efficiently, and they can also prevent injury.

A baseball player with an awkward swing can hurt their back more easily than someone with a more horizontal swing. A batter that has to pull harder with their arms and their back when using a heavier bat is subject to injury, too. Many sports teams use video to record each player's standard movement, then go over it with them. This helps them to not only improve their performance but also to keep them safe.

But it's not just the video that helps. Computers evaluate each movement the baseball player makes. The computer analyzes the angles of the arms, the hips, the legs. It can tell the trainer if the player is using their body to the best advantage to get the most power.

The computer makes suggestions to the trainer for ways to help the player become more efficient with their swing. Or perhaps to get more power from their release. This use of technology has helped players to make great strides in their performance, as well as keeping them safe.

LOOKING AHEAD

With technology, there is always something more exciting on the horizon. What's next for sporting equipment? Graphene. It, too, is a form of carbon (did you guess that?). Graphene is even stronger than carbon nanotubes. Yet it is so thin that a single layer of graphene is invisible to the human eye. Graphene is cool! It is stronger than steel and diamonds, too. It is also extremely lightweight, and yet more flexible than a rubber ball. Wait. This is strong, light, and bendable? Sounds too good to be true. It isn't. Graphene was discovered in 2010, and scientists and engineers have been working to find ways to use it ever since.

WHAT IS GRAPHENE?

GRAPHENE SOUNDS LIKE something from a sci-fi movie, doesn't it? And yet, you probably have a variation of this amazing substance sitting right on your desk. Have a pencil? That is made of graphite. Well, graphene and graphite are the same thing! That's right. Your pencil is actually made up of many layers of graphene. Those layers come together to make up graphite. Graphite is found in metamorphic rocks (rocks that have been subjected to high heat and pressure) in different parts of the world. Look for them in South America, Asia, and North America.

Did you know that graphite, graphene, and diamonds are all related? They are all made of carbon atoms. What makes them different? How they are arranged. Graphene is a single layer of graphite. Its atoms are arranged in a 2-dimensional structure. *2-D* means that it's flat, like any words you might draw on a piece of paper. Diamonds are made of a carbon structure that is 3-dimensional, or 3-D. Something that is 3-D has length, width, and depth. Like a pencil, or a chair, or even this whole book. Unfortunately for you, though, arrangement is everything. Your bit of graphite pencil? It's not worth as much as a diamond. Too bad, isn't it?

Companies are really excited at the prospect of using graphene in their sports equipment. Tennis rackets are getting lighter because of graphene. From the 1870s to the 1970s, tennis rackets were made of wood. They were also more circular in shape and had strings that were tough and didn't give a lot. Compared to today's rackets, they were heavy and a bit clumsy to use.

That was before the discovery of carbon fiber technology and now graphene. Tennis manufacturers now use graphene in all parts of their rackets. From the strings, to the frame, to even the grip where you put your hand. The frames are wider and more oval-shaped to allow for a "sweet spot." The sweet spot is considered the best place on the racket to hit the ball. This spot sends the ball soaring across the net as fast as possible and directly to the place where you want it to land. Lightweight and flexible, these new graphene tennis rackets are supposed to feel like an extension of your hand. Well, if your hand were able to hit something over 150 mph, that is. Whoosh!

If you love to ski, you'll probably be doing so on skis enhanced with graphene, too. Snow skis used to be made with wood and glass fibers, but now manufacturers are adding a few layers of graphene to the ski. Skis are now made using a thin wood block that is sandwiched in the middle as the base, but on the top and bottom are glass fibers and a layer or two of graphene to add strength. This makes the ski stronger, more flexible, and lighter. Remember that combination? It means you have to use less energy to move. Which means you can fly down the mountain. Be sure you have your poles ready to help steer!

Let's not forget safety. Graphene can also be found in new bike helmets. Safety is important in every sport, particularly cycling. Wearing a helmet is essential when you are speeding down a mountain at 30 mph or even while navigating dogs and people on a sidewalk in your neighborhood. Good thing companies have created new graphene-enhanced bike helmets to keep you safe. These helmets are designed with graphene nanofibers in what's called a roll cage. Think of it as sort of a safety "cage" for your head. The helmet roll cage is strong, hopefully enough to protect your head from major injury if you happen to be catapulted over the handlebars. The best part is, it's light and comfortable,

IS USING TECHNOLOGY IN SPORTS EQUIPMENT FAIR?

THIS IS A good question, but also a tough one to answer. Clearly sports equipment has gotten better over the years. For example, football helmets used in the 1930s were made of leather.

Those were not really safe for the player, and they didn't help to prevent concussions at all. The football helmets of the 2020s are layered with different materials to cushion and protect players from injury. That is definitely a good advance in sports technology.

But what if the technology actually improves an athlete's performance? Golf balls made with nanotechnology are able to fly faster and farther than before. Even with the same effort of swing from the athlete. The same goes for tennis balls, which are now made bouncier and lighter. Tennis players can send them flying across the net at speeds that weren't possible before.

Then there's the question of cost. The prices of equipment made with advanced technology tend to be much higher than all the rest. Is technology only for athletes who can afford it?

which means it's more likely people will wear it. After all, it can only protect you if you have it on. (Hint: Wear helmets when you go biking!).

Many other companies are working on ways to use graphene in their sports equipment, too. As technology continues to improve, you'll see more of this equipment. Who knows? Maybe someday there will even be a graphene swimsuit. One that will make you fly through the water. Of course, the best way to get faster at swimming? Practice! (Yep, I went there.)

The answer to these questions is a tough one. And one that is hotly debated among athletes and sports analysts. This would make for a great discussion. What do you think?

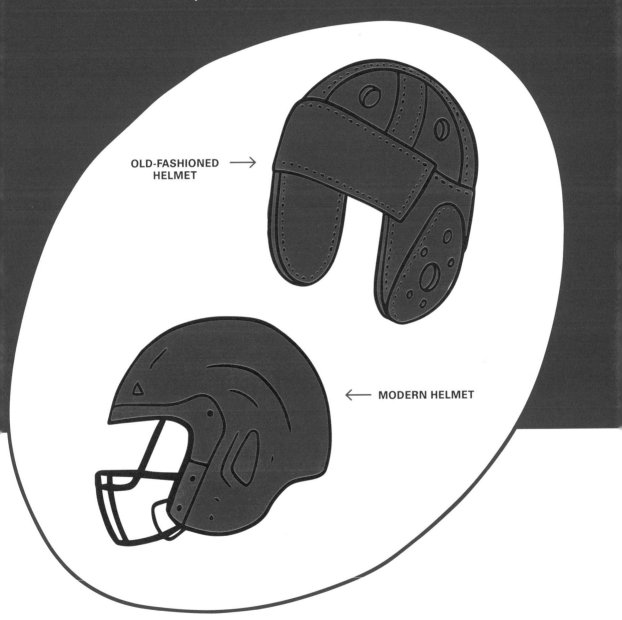

OLD-FASHIONED HELMET →

← MODERN HELMET

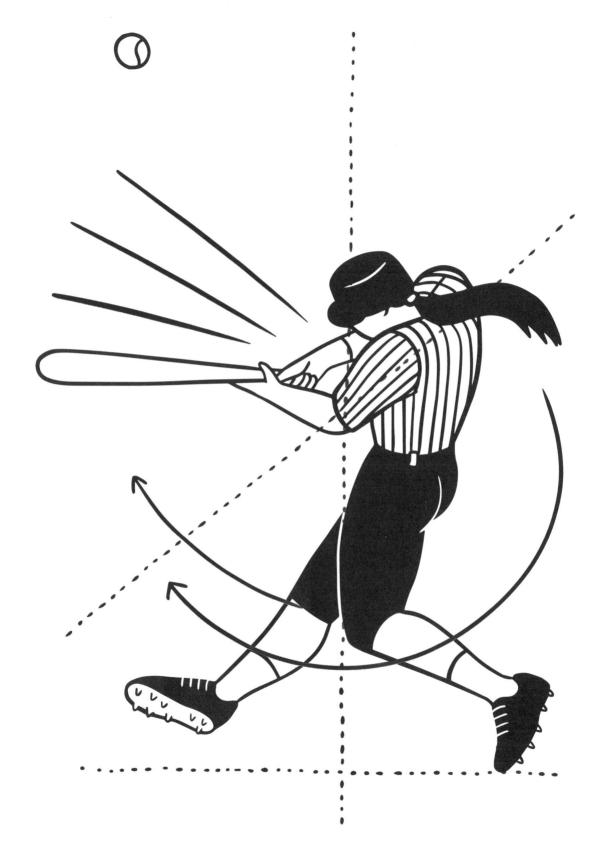

CHAPTER 3 ENGINEERING A WIN

YOU NOW KNOW how to prepare your body for participating in sports—and also how technology keeps you safe and helps increase your performance. It's time to put all of that science into action. Let's talk about how we can use engineering to help us win. Winning is definitely not everything, but it *is* nice when it happens. Is there a secret science to help you win? Yes. Of course, let's not forget that working hard and staying fit and healthy are important, too. But if you had the chance to use science and engineering to increase your performance, you would do it, wouldn't you? Sure you would.

In this section you will learn about forces, movement, and how physics plays a huge part in the design of sports equipment. Did you know that footballs were once round? That at one time pitchers made their own baseballs? And soccer balls were originally made out of inflated pig bladders or balls stuffed with feathers? Sounds weird, doesn't it?

Clearly things have changed in the many years since those sports started. The real questions are: How did these balls evolve? And why were new ones created? (Hint: It wasn't just because it got tough to find pig bladders.) The answer is physics.

Understanding physics, which is the science and property of matter in space and time, is important when you are playing sports. It's not just helpful in determining the shape of the ball, but in pretty much all aspects of a sport. Do you play a sport where you hit, kick, or catch a ball? You can use physics to predict where the ball will go, where it will land, and if it will make it into the hoop or net. It also tells you how to best dodge and weave around a person who is bent on tackling you.

Physics and engineering go together very well. Engineers use the principle of physics to design sports equipment that cuts down on the forces of lift, drag, and friction. An important goal that not only sends your ball flying through the air faster, it also teaches you the most efficient way to run, swim, dive, and so on. Sounds like it might be a good idea to take a closer look at how physics and engineering can help you become a better athlete.

PHYSICS IS YOUR FRIEND

Before diving into the ins and outs of how to improve your play, let's start with some basic physics. First, you need to know Newton's Laws of Motion. Do you remember them from your science or physics class? If not, you can review them quickly here.

NEWTON'S FIRST LAW OF MOTION

An object at rest will stay at rest until acted upon. An object in motion will stay in motion until acted upon.

NEWTON'S FIRST LAW OF MOTION

AN OBJECT AT REST WILL REMAIN AT REST . . .

UNTIL ACTED UPON BY AN UNBALANCED FORCE.

AN OBJECT IN MOTION WILL CONTINUE WITH CONSTANT SPEED AND DIRECTION . . .

UNTIL ACTED ON BY AN UNBALANCED FORCE.

How does this work in sports? Soccer is a great example of this. A soccer ball that is still on the grass will not move until it is kicked. A soccer ball that is moving across the grass will not stop until it is stopped by an object.

That is technically correct; however, another force is involved when an object is moving across a surface. It is called friction. Friction affects all moving objects (unless they are on a frictionless surface).

FRICTION FACTOR

FRICTION IS THE force that slows down a moving object. It acts in the opposite direction to the way the object is moving.

For example, if you kicked a soccer ball to the right, the friction force moves to the left, against the ball. As the ball rolls, friction slows the ball's momentum ever so slightly until finally the ball comes to a stop.

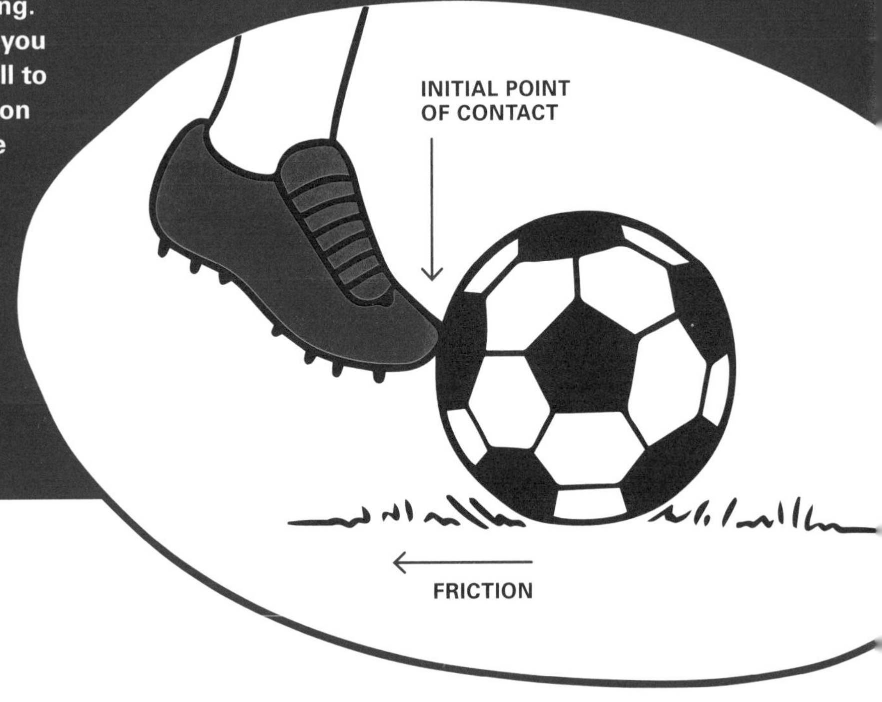

INITIAL POINT OF CONTACT

FRICTION

Wait. That sounds like it's contradicting Newton's First Law. Nope. Actually, friction is an outside force that is acting on the object. So, just like the law says, friction is acting on the object so it slows down. If there weren't any friction, the ball would keep rolling. That's true. But on Earth it is impossible (at least right now) to have a frictionless surface. What about in space, where there is very little gravity? Yep. There is friction there, too. Although the friction in space is much, much smaller than here on Earth.

NEWTON'S SECOND LAW OF MOTION
The force on an object is equal to the object's mass times its acceleration (or speed).

Which in basic terms means that if something has more mass, or weighs a lot, it's going to take a lot more force to move it. That makes sense. Have you ever tried to pick up a really heavy box? It takes a lot of energy or force, right? You have to strain your muscles and pull really hard to lift it. But a box that is light is easy to pick up and move. You can probably even slide it easily across the floor.

Apply that same idea to sports. If something is lighter, and you give it a really big kick (or force) it's going to accelerate very rapidly away

from you. This is important in sports because the mass or weight of a piece of equipment determines how far it will go when you apply a force. Footballs and soccer balls tend to be light; that means if you put a lot of force behind your throw or kick, they will go far. But baseballs, lacrosse balls, and hockey pucks are heavier and have more mass. They need a lot of force to get them to fly through the air. That is why the batter or hockey player pulls back their bat or stick really far before hitting the ball or puck. The action of pulling back their arm gives them a greater force for striking the object.

NEWTON'S THIRD LAW OF MOTION
For every action there is an equal and opposite reaction.

You've already learned about this in previous chapters. Remember? It means every time you push on something it pushes back on you. To be clear, it's not always an actual push back at you. When your foot hits the ground as you run, the ground doesn't push back on your foot. What is really happening is that the same force you are directing into the ground with your foot comes back from the ground into your foot. Still confused? Take a look at the diagram.

The force from your foot goes into the ground (that is, the gravitational

GROUND REACTION FORCE

FORCE FROM YOUR FOOT GOING INTO THE GROUND

force times your weight). The force from the ground, called the normal force, is the ground reaction force. It travels through your foot and up your leg.

Now that you know how the laws of physics work, it's time to use them to your advantage. Sports is pretty much all about physics. That is why using engineering can help you to brainstorm, design, and create the most efficient sports equipment. You can also use engineering to figure out the best place to stand to catch a ball.

FORCEFUL RETURNS

Ready to use the knowledge you have about forces? Great. Grab a racket, bat, or club, and let's get going. You are going to experience Newton's First and Second Laws firsthand. You already know that an object in motion will stay in motion unless acted upon. Let's apply that to the game of tennis. In tennis, the object is to get the ball across the net before it bounces twice on your side of the court.

During a game, tennis balls are in constant motion. They bounce off rackets, the ground, and even the net. Every time the ball hits something, a tiny bit of its energy is transferred to that object. The loss of that energy causes the ball to slow unless more force is added to the ball. This happens when the player returns the ball. This is where Newton's Second Law comes in. The amount of force applied to the ball is directly proportional to the acceleration of the ball. In easy terms, it means that if you whack the ball really hard, you will send it flying at a high speed across the net. Tennis players use this knowledge to keep their opponents on their toes, quite literally.

How can tennis players engineer a great shot? Typically, the hardest shots to return are the ones that are really strong and fast. A tennis player gets the power behind their serve by pulling their arm (the one with the racket) backward and then sweeping it forward very fast. When the racket connects with the ball...*Bam!* The powerful shot flies across the net (assuming they aimed it properly, anyway). The arm position that many players use for returning shots occurs when their arm is parallel (or almost parallel) to the ground. Can't imagine this? Take a look at the image.

This tennis player is putting as much energy as she can into this swing. You can see the effort on her face. This ball probably flew across the net. Wonder what the speed of the ball was? Some tennis players have serves that are as fast as 106 mph or higher. Talk about speedy!

How are professional tennis players able to hit the ball that hard and fast? Practice! And also, they use a

ARM
PARALLEL
TO THE
GROUND

bit of physics and engineering. When you pull back a lever before you use it, you are making stored energy, which is released all at once as you swing. This creates a larger force than if you don't pull your arm back. Tennis players do it, baseball pitchers do it, and lacrosse players and volleyball players each wind up their arm to throw or hit the ball. This is because their arm is a simple machine called a lever. Levers give lots of power when you pull them back first to get more energy.

WHAT IS A LEVER?

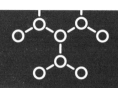

A LEVER IS known as a simple machine. Simple machines are devices with very few moving parts. Actually some of them, like a wedge, don't have any moving parts. They are used to help people do work. You have several simple machines in your body. Your arms and legs are levers. Your teeth act as wedges as they grind down your food.

A lever has 2 main parts: a long beam and a fulcrum (or pivot).

The beam is the long, straight part of the lever. The fulcrum or pivot is the point where the lever moves. The load is what you are moving.

When you are playing tennis, your arm is a lever. The forearm is the beam, and your elbow is the fulcrum.

Of course, your shoulder can also be a fulcrum. In golf, players keep their arms straight to hit the ball. That means their shoulder is the fulcrum and the entire arm is their beam. Bet you never thought of yourself as being a simple machine. You are!

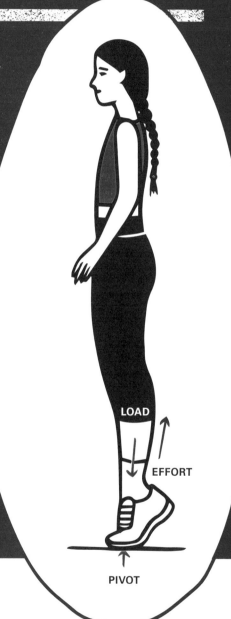

LOAD

EFFORT

PIVOT

EFFORT

PIVOT

LOAD

Play baseball? You already know all about levers. Your arm is the lever that gives you the big power to hit the ball. *Whack!*

Your arm or shoulder provides the power to your swing. Is there a way to increase that power? Yes. Plant your feet first. Think about a tennis player: When you see them get ready to return a serve, what do they do first? They may run over or lunge to get their racket behind the ball. Then they plant their feet, pull their arm(s) back, and swing forward as fast and hard as they can. Baseball players are taught to do the same thing. You step into the batter's box, plant your feet a small distance apart, then pull your bat around and behind your shoulder and wait for the pitch. When you are ready to swing, you step forward on your front foot and lean into the swing. The act of planting your feet and leaning in adds power to your swing. Next time you are at a baseball game, watch the batter to see if they do that.

Lacrosse, badminton, Ping-Pong, and squash players all plant their feet and then swing. Why? So that you have a strong base to bring your arm around as fast and as hard as you can.

Can you swing without planting your feet? Sure. But it won't be as hard as if you planted them first. Not sure? Test it out.

BATTER UP!

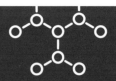

FIND A SAFE place to test this out, away from homes, windows, and other people. Use a plastic baseball bat and a plastic ball. Get a friend. Stand up to a plate or just a piece of grass. Have your friend step back about 10 feet. Then have them pitch to you. Plant your feet. Take a swing. See how far the baseball flies.

Try it again, but this time do not plant your feet. Take a swing. Did the ball go as far as the first time? And how difficult was it to not plant your feet before your swing? Probably pretty tough. It's instinct to dig in and get yourself stable before swinging.

What most athletes have learned is that if they put a huge amount of power behind their shot, it will accelerate rapidly. It will also most likely travel farther. The real question, however, is: Where will it land? For that, continue reading this chapter to learn how objects soar through the air. (Hint: It's a very uplifting section.)

What most athletes have learned is that if they put a huge amount of power behind their shot, it will accelerate rapidly. It will also most likely travel farther. The real question, however, is: Where will it land? For that, continue reading this chapter to learn how objects soar through the air. (Hint: It's a very uplifting section.)

BALL-ISTICS
Have you ever played catch with someone? What do you notice when you throw a ball? Does it travel in a straight line? Nope. It curves. Don't believe me? Give it a try.

CURVING BALL TEST

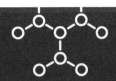

GO OUTSIDE AND bring a friend with you. Find a safe place to throw a football back and forth. Stand about 10 feet apart. Throw the football to your friend. As the football flies, notice that it goes up slightly in a curve as it travels toward your friend. If you have a hard time seeing this, go get another friend. Have the two of them throw the football back and forth while you stand back and watch. Notice that the ball follows a curved path. It looks like the illustration below.

Now have your friend kick the ball. Watch what happens to the football. You guessed it—it curves, too.

No matter what type of object you throw, kick, or hit, as long as it's put into motion in the same manner, it will follow a curved path. (An exception would be a Frisbee, but then you are "throwing" the Frisbee in a different way from a ball, so that doesn't count.)

So why does the object follow a curved path? It has to do with gravity.

WHAT IS GRAVITY?

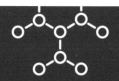

IT IS THE force that pulls everything on Earth to its center. The force is measured in terms of acceleration, or meters per second squared (m/s^2). If you assume that any object moving upward has a positive acceleration (+), then anything moving downward must have a negative acceleration (−). Gravity on the Earth is −9.8 m/s^2.

You can't escape gravity. At least not here on the Earth. Gravity is different for every celestial body. For example, gravity on the Moon is about $1/6$ the gravity here on Earth, or only 1.62 m/s^2. Gravity affects the weight of an object. As gravity increases, so does the weight. You might weigh 100 pounds here on Earth, but on the Moon you will weigh only 16.5 pounds. Gravity does not affect the mass of an object. If your mass is 100 pounds on the Earth, it will still be 100 pounds on the Moon.

Let's go back to the football. When you throw a football into the air, the ball accelerates upward, but also forward and horizontally to the ground. If you were on the Moon, where there is very little gravity, the ball would travel a great distance before falling. On the Earth, things are different. The instant the ball leaves your hand, gravity begins to act on the football, pulling it to the ground. Even though the football wants to travel upward and horizontally, the longer the ball travels, the greater the force of gravity becomes. You can see when gravity starts to "win" because that is when the ball begins to curve downward. Eventually, gravity wins, and the ball lands on the ground.

This type of movement is called projectile motion. And it happens in every sport with a ball: baseball, basketball, tennis, lacrosse, golf, volleyball, and so on. Balls that are thrown, kicked, or hit travel along this same projectile motion track.

Why do we care about this? Well, if you are going to use engineering to help you play better, you will want to understand how projectile motion works. If you can learn to predict how far a ball will travel, then you can anticipate the exact point where it will land. A baseball player will then catch the ball, a golfer will hit the ball into the cup, and a volleyball player will be in the right spot to make a great return. See how engineering and physics help you? Bet you're paying attention now. Here is the part where you learn how to be a better player.

WHERE WILL IT LAND?

Projectiles are thrown or kicked into the air and typically follow a parabola, or curved path. The distance a ball travels depends on two things: the force of the throw and the angle of the throw. The force is determined by how hard you throw it. Do you wind your arm way back and put your entire body into the throw? That will put a very large force behind the ball. Its initial speed or velocity will be great. A high velocity will make the ball travel farther. You already know that from learning about Newton's Second Law. But did you know that the angle of the throw is just as important as the velocity? It is. The angle of the throw tells you how far the ball will travel in the air. There are many ways that you can angle the ball.

- If you throw the ball straight up, it will come almost straight down.

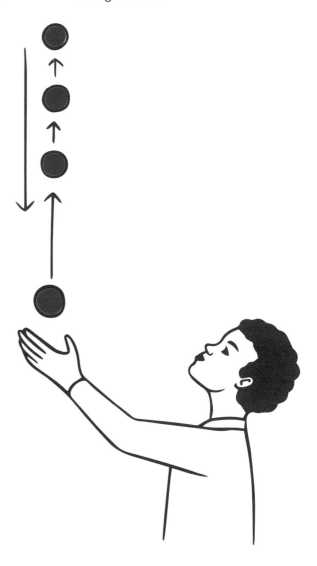

- If you throw the ball upward and forward, it will take longer to fall back to the ground, and thus it will travel a longer distance.

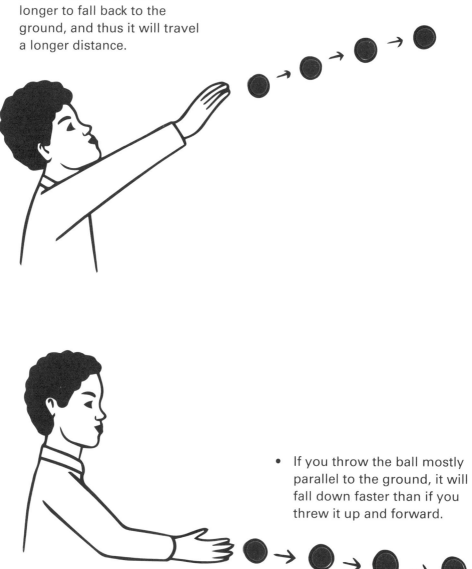

- If you throw the ball mostly parallel to the ground, it will fall down faster than if you threw it up and forward.

- If you angle the ball toward the ground, it will naturally fall to the ground quickly.

This same idea works for kicking a ball.

When you are throwing a ball, your height is a factor in how far the ball travels, too, since that is its initial height. It makes sense. If the ball starts at a certain height off the ground, it has that much farther to travel before it falls down. This is also one of the reasons why football quarterbacks and baseball pitchers are usually around six feet tall. The extra height gives the ball the advantage of traveling a greater distance, and it allows quarterbacks to see over the linemen, who can often be well over six feet tall.

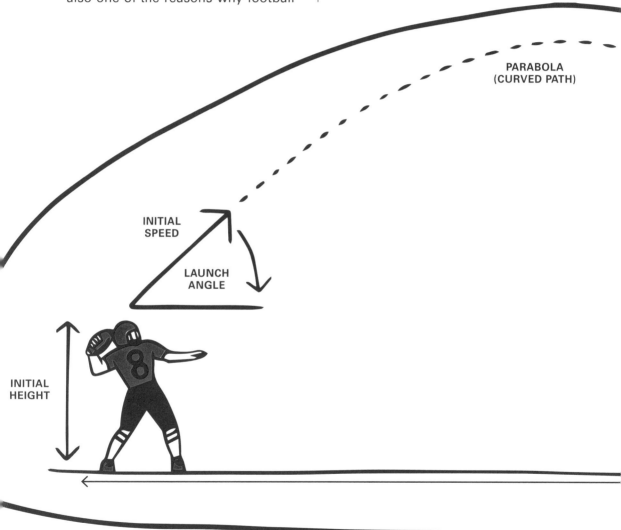

PARABOLA
(CURVED PATH)

INITIAL
SPEED

LAUNCH
ANGLE

INITIAL
HEIGHT

THROWING PRACTICE

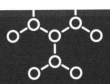

TIME TO TRY this out again. Go get that football and 2 of your friends. Watch them as they toss the ball back and forth. But this time, have them change the angle and velocity of their throws. You watch what happens to the ball. First have 1 friend throw the ball really hard and at a shorter angle. Then have them throw it softly and at a higher angle. Notice what the person who is catching has to do. It might surprise you. Do this a couple of times to see if you can find a pattern.

Did you notice that changing the angle and the speed of the football affected the person trying to catch it? They probably had to move back and forth, and maybe even side to side, to catch the ball. They could no longer stay in the same place as they had before when they were playing catch. Were they able to catch every football that was thrown to them? If so, how?

RANGE

VELOCITY

The best way to predict where the ball will land is to follow its apex. That is the highest point in the curve of the parabola. Once the ball hits that point, it will curve more rapidly to the ground. That is because at that point the force of gravity has slowed the velocity enough that the ball loses

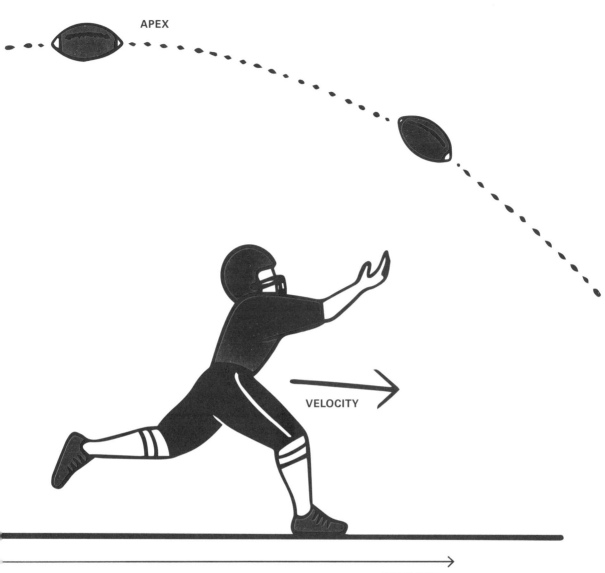

speed. The loss in speed causes the ball to lose height and distance.

Want to be a great player? Learn to find the apex of the throw. By following the curve at the apex down with your eye, you can figure out where the ball is going to land. The trick is to get there before it does.

This is not always easy to do. Have you ever watched a football game where passes were dropped? Or a baseball game where they missed a catch? That can happen if the person can't get to the place where the ball will land and catch it before it hits the ground.

Hitting a moving target, like a running player, requires lots of practice! Whether you are on a football, lacrosse, baseball, or basketball team, practice is needed so that players can learn where to go. Multiple hours a day are spent just throwing and catching passes. You can try this with your friend. Run out, do a zigzag, turn around, and catch the ball. Did you do it? Great. Try it again, and again. Make different moves. Have the person throw the ball at different velocities. It's not as easy as it looks to catch the ball every time, is it?

For that you'll need to work on your reaction time, which is the amount of time it takes to respond to a stimulus. In this case, to run fast enough to catch the ball before it lands. You must learn to gauge your speed against the distance you need to travel. For example, if your friend is aiming to throw the ball twenty feet away, how long will it take you to get there before the ball? It depends on where you are standing. Are you next to your friend or ten feet in front of him? Ten feet behind him? And how hard is your friend throwing the ball? All of that matters in the reaction time.

If you've ever watched football players running out to catch a pass, you will see them sprint, or run as fast as they can to get to their spot. They know exactly how far to go forward, then they turn back for the catch. The quarterback knows exactly when to throw the ball to get to the receiver just in time. It looks very easy, but it's actually quite complicated. Each of the players must move in the same manner every time in order to make this catch happen with ease. The reaction time of the receiver is very important. If he takes off more slowly, he won't get there before the ball does. If he takes off too fast, he will be there before the ball, and he may be stuck waiting for it. A receiver wants to be able to turn, catch the ball, and keep running with it. They don't want to be standing still waiting for the football. That leaves them open to being tackled.

TESTING YOUR REACTION TIME

WANT TO TEST your reaction time? Get back outside with a friend and a stopwatch or your cell phone. You need something that will measure time, preferably in minutes and seconds. Mark out a space that is anywhere between 10 and 50 feet across (use a tape measure). It's better if you have a longer area if possible. Pick one end as your start. The other end is your finish.

Have your friend get ready with the timer. Get ready to run: 3…2…1…GO! Run as fast as you can to the finish line. Have your friend record your time. That is how fast your reaction time is. If you want to improve, then you have to…practice. You knew I was going to say that, didn't you? But seriously, this is what athletes do to improve their performance; they practice their reaction times to make themselves faster.

SWINGING FOR THE FENCES

Do you play baseball? If so, maybe you've hit a home run, or two. Did you ever stop to think about all the physics that are involved in that one swing? How are you able to hit the ball so high and so far? The answer comes down to a couple of things. First, there is ballistics. You've already learned that to increase the distance that a ball travels, you need to start with a higher arc. Of course, that doesn't mean you want to hit the ball straight up into the air. That will result in a pop fly and will likely end in an out for your team. When you hit the ball, you want it to soar upward in a high, curving arc. Take a look at the drawing as an example.

The second part of being a good hitter is impact. The impact of your bat on the ball plays a big part in how high and far the ball will fly. You want to hit the ball as hard as you can. But there's something else to think about: the sweet spot. Every bat has one. What's the sweet spot? It's the place on the bat where the ball will get the most energy from your swing. Keep

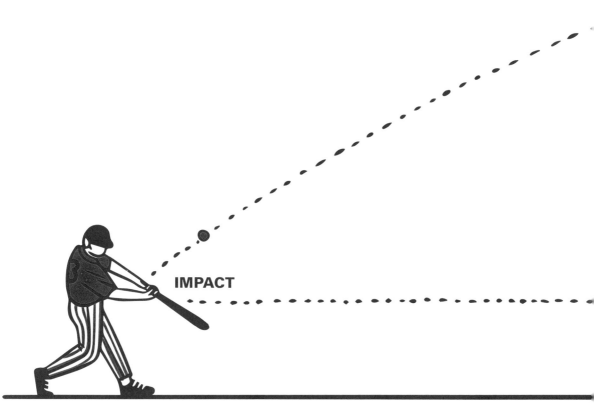

IMPACT

in mind, the sweet spot is not a single point on the bat, it's more like a small area or zone that is the best place on the bat to hit the ball.

When the ball and bat collide, the bat vibrates with the impact. These vibrations are transferred to the ball, and also to your hand. The goal is to get most of these vibrations to transfer to the ball *instead of* your hand.

More vibrations = more energy. Physicists have figured out that there is a sweet spot on every bat. If you hit the ball in this zone, the majority of the vibrations will transfer to the ball.

The sweet spot is located toward the end of the bat. You want to hit the ball in between those two lines for maximum power.

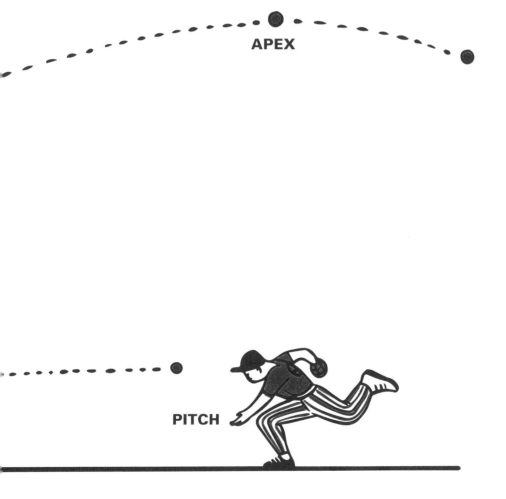

APEX

PITCH

FINDING THE SWEET SPOT ON YOUR BAT

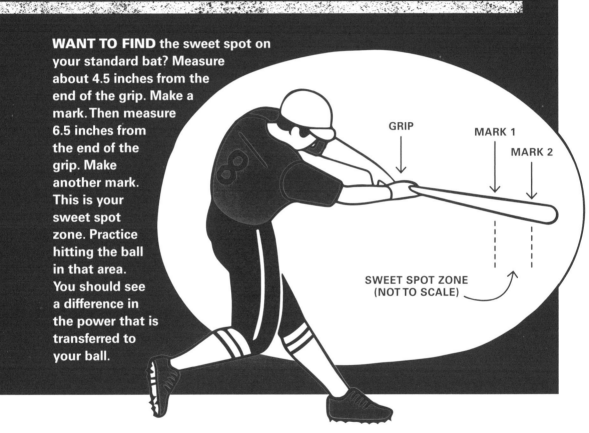

WANT TO FIND the sweet spot on your standard bat? Measure about 4.5 inches from the end of the grip. Make a mark. Then measure 6.5 inches from the end of the grip. Make another mark. This is your sweet spot zone. Practice hitting the ball in that area. You should see a difference in the power that is transferred to your ball.

GRIP

MARK 1

MARK 2

SWEET SPOT ZONE
(NOT TO SCALE)

The third idea that you need to understand in order to hit home runs is reaction timing. Just as tennis players need to understand when to pull their racket back before swinging, baseball players need to do the same thing with their bat. Think about how you stand at home plate. You have your shoulders set up to the side of the plate. You are looking over either your right or left shoulder (depending on if you are right- or left-handed). One foot is in front of the other, your feet are wide apart, and your bat is pulled back over your shoulder. Your eyes are focused on the pitcher and the baseball in their hand. You are ready to swing.

The real question is, how fast will that ball be coming toward you? This matters because in order to connect with the ball, your bat needs to be in a certain position to hit it. In a matter of a few seconds, your brain must assess the speed of the ball, how fast it's traveling toward you, and its angle, then give directions to your muscles to move your bat around quickly enough to hit the ball. That sounds complicated. But that is why baseball players practice batting over and over.

As you get used to estimating the speed and angle of a throw, you'll be able to hit the ball more often. Also, perhaps you'll even start to hit the ball in the bat's sweet spot. Let's take a look at how this works.

A major league pitcher is throwing the ball at you at 90 miles per hour. You are standing 60 feet away at home plate. You have 400 milliseconds to hit the ball before it goes across the plate. What do you do?

- Your eyes have 100 milliseconds to see the ball.

- Your brain takes up to 75 milliseconds to determine the speed and angle of the ball.

- You have 25 milliseconds to decide if you're going to hit the ball or let it go by.

- If you decide to swing, you must start your swing NOW— it takes 150 milliseconds to swing your bat around to where the ball will be.

- *THWACK!*

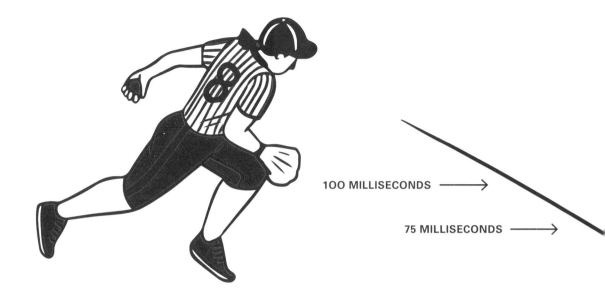

100 MILLISECONDS ⟶

75 MILLISECONDS ⟶

Here are the possible outcomes that may occur:

1. You did it! You hit the ball in the sweet spot, and it soared over the head of the outfielders. Home run!

2. Swing and a miss. It's strike one for you.

3. You swing and get a hit that sends you to a base.

4. You swing and your ball goes out of bounds, and is called a foul ball.

5. You hit the ball and it is caught. You are out.

6. You don't swing at all, and you get either a strike or a ball called on you.

All this took a little over four hundred milliseconds. That is about the same amount of time it takes to blink your eye. That is fast! No wonder baseball players practice batting so much. It's all about the timing. If you are even a few milliseconds early or late with your swing, you will miss the ball with your bat.

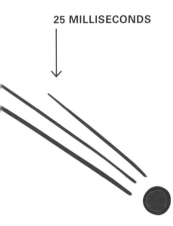

25 MILLISECONDS

TARGET PRACTICE

What happens if you're not trying to catch or hit the ball being thrown at you? Maybe you want to just hit the ball to a certain spot. You still want to watch the apex of the shot. But honestly, it's also important to figure out the angle and the velocity of the shot in order to reach the exact point where you want the ball to land.

Let's use soccer for this example. Say you want to kick the ball into the goal. What is important to know? Where you are. Where the goal is. The angle from you to the goal. Also if there are any players between you and the goal. You will need to think carefully about this—and quickly, too, if you are in a game. Remember that the higher you kick the ball, the less distance it will travel. So, if you are close to the net, you may want to aim higher. This will give you a short shot and will also (hopefully) clear any defensive players who might be in your way. The trick is to get the ball to fall when you want it to. That means practicing to get the apex of your shot just right.

Of course, there is always something else to consider. This time it's where your kick occurs on the ball. That's right. You can change the angle, the velocity, and the spin on a ball based on where you kick it. A kick low to the ground where you move your leg upward will send the ball higher into the air. If you put a lot of force behind it, the ball may have a large parabola and travel a lot of distance. Putting a bit less force behind it will cause the ball to go up, but not quite as high. This will create a shorter parabola. It may be just perfect to use this kick to get the ball over the defender's head before it drops on the ground, and hopefully into the goal.

Kicking the ball directly in the middle will most likely keep it on the ground. A good solid kick in the middle of the ball is a perfect way to pass the ball to your teammate. Or maybe, if you're lucky, to get a goal.

BEND IT LIKE BECKHAM

SOMETIMES THE WAY to get the best angle on a shot in soccer is to bend yourself. This sounds weird, but keep reading. The position of your foot when it connects with the ball plays a part in where the ball goes. What if instead of kicking the ball straight on, you bend your body and your foot at a weird angle to kick the ball? You may be able to get just enough spin on the ball to have it sailing over the goalie's head and into the far corner of the net. Watch some professional soccer players. They have made some amazing goals using their bodies as part of the "equipment."

MAKING SOME HOOPS

Basketball is another sport where you are trying to get a ball to hit a certain target. In this case, you want the basketball to go through the hoop. This is not as easy as it looks. Especially because when you are shooting the basketball, you may be anywhere on the court. Many things go into making a basket—your hands' position on the ball, the force and angle of your shot, even how high you jump as you shoot. It all comes down to physics.

Today, the size and shape of a basketball is standard, but it hasn't always been this way. The very first basketball games were played with soccer balls. These balls were not very bouncy and they didn't work well. So a new basketball was designed. It had a circumference (the distance around the entire ball) of thirty-two inches, or four inches bigger than a soccer ball. The outside was made of leather and it had an inflatable rubber bladder inside. At first, basketballs were brown, but players complained they were too hard to see. So, the color was changed to orange.

Today's standard basketball has a circumference of 29.5 inches (75 centimeters). That makes it large enough for a person to handle it with one hand while they are bouncing it. It's large, but not too large. Imagine if a basketball were smaller, like the size of a soccer ball or tennis ball. It would be more difficult to handle with one hand. You might miss getting your hand on the smaller ball. With a basketball, you can keep your hand in the same place and bounce it sometimes without even thinking about it. (The best professionals can bounce a basketball while they are doing many other things—looking around at other players, at the basket, or even at the sidelines).

Being able to control the ball with one hand is very important when you go to shoot it. It allows you to focus on what really matters in a shot—ballistics. Remember the apex of the shooting arc? It's very important when you are shooting a basketball. As you let go of your shot, follow the arc of the ball with your eyes. Try to estimate the position of the apex, so that you can determine where the ball will come down. (Hint: Preferably in the hoop.)

Basketball hoops are eighteen inches in diameter. The backboard is 42 inches high and 72 inches wide and is located 10 feet off the ground. While we aren't going to do the calculations here (that will be in the next chapter), you do need to have a feel for the height of the hoop when you are shooting the ball. Making a shot

depends on the angle and the amount of energy you put into your shot.

Remember, the basket is higher than you are. To get your shot even higher and give it some lift, you will need to add some height. Since you can't add five-inch heels to your basketball shoes, you'll have to jump.

Bending your knees and jumping up can add anywhere from six to eighteen inches to your overall height. The trick is to let go of the ball when you are at the peak of your jump. That will give your ball the lift it needs to fly into the air.

There is a method to shooting a basketball that will help you get the correct angle. Typically, you shoot with your dominant hand. Are you left-handed or right-handed? Whichever one you write with is your dominant hand.

NOTHING BUT NET

Are you ready to put this all into action? Here's the secret science behind a great basketball shot. Put your dominant hand on the back of the ball. Take your other hand and place it on the side of the ball. The hand on the side doesn't really touch the ball, it just helps you to guide your shot. Bend the wrist of your dominant hand back toward your body. Push your hand forward as hard and as fast as you can. Let your hand naturally go all the way forward. That

BEND THE WRIST OF YOUR DOMINANT HAND BACK TOWARD YOUR BODY

DOMINANT HAND ON THE BACK OF THE BALL AND OTHER HAND ON SIDE OF THE BALL

PUSH YOUR HAND FORWARD

is called the follow-through, and it's an important part of the shot. As your fingertips leave the ball, they are still helping to direct it to the right place. Wherever you are on the court, position yourself at an angle to the hoop and shoot.

Note that the harder you push the ball away from yourself during the shot, the farther it will fly. The higher the angle you make with your hands, the higher the ball will go up.

Hopefully, the ball goes in. As they say, "Nothing but net." You can, of course, bounce the ball off the backboard. That is another way to get a shot through the hoop. You'll learn more about that in the next chapter. Understanding math and geometry specifically can really help your basketball game.

PRACTICE YOUR SHOT

GRAB A BASKETBALL and head to the nearest court. Or anywhere with a hoop. Don't have a hoop? Make a circle on the ground or pick a spot on the wall and aim there. Take some time to move around the court and shoot the basketball. Try to make it into the hoop. Be sure to go to each side of the court. Do you have a favorite? Some players do. They like to take shots on the left side or the right side. But the best players can take shots from anywhere on the court. Over time, you'll get a feel for the basketball and how hard you have to push to shoot it, plus what angles are the best for you.

THE SCIENCE OF
THE SLAM DUNK

If you've ever watched a basketball game, you've seen a slam dunk. Let's face it, they are cool! One person jumps up, appears to lift the ball over the rim, then jams it down through the hoop. DUNK! You'd really like to know how to do that, wouldn't you?

Just like everything else, it's all about physics. A slam dunk is different from a regular shot. A slam dunk requires you to jump, move forward, lift your arm high, and aim the ball into the corner of the board or right into the basket. This happens in a few seconds. You blink, and it's over. Well, not quite, but close. First, there's the jump. That is a bit of Newton's Third Law in action. As the player's foot pushes hard off the floor, the opposite energy is pushed up into their legs. Players use a big step and push to propel themselves high into the air. As they are going up, however, they are also going forward. The idea is to cover a lot of ground with this jump, to get closer to the basket without taking steps on the floor. Obviously, as the player leaves the floor, gravity begins to act upon them, pulling them back down. So the player lifts up their arm, holding the basketball in one hand, and stretches as far as they can. The player must time it right so that they reach the apex of the jump just when they are at the height of the basket. Or at least where their hand can lift the basketball up and over the rim. Swoosh! The ball goes in as the player lands heavily on the floor (gravity finally having caught up with them).

Sound fun? It is. Dunking a basketball is tons of fun. It's not easy to do, though. You need to be fairly tall or have an incredibly high vertical leap...or both.

MECHANICS: SHAPES
MAKE THE SPORT

Did you ever stop to think about all the different shapes used in sports? Most of the balls are round. Golf balls, basketballs, tennis balls, soccer balls, and lacrosse balls are all round. It sort of makes sense, since round-shaped balls travel along more predictable paths. They can spin, but typically their flight is much more controlled. A round ball also bounces better. They are able to bounce up and down with one hand or racket.

BOUNCY IS BETTER

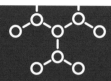

IF YOU'VE PLAYED basketball, tennis, or lacrosse, you have probably played with a flat ball on occasion. A flat ball is a ball that doesn't have enough air in it. Flat balls don't bounce and they are harder to hit. They don't go as far as you want, or where you want. Let's face it, playing with a flat ball stinks.

Why is that? The bouncier a ball is, the faster it will move. Speed is important in pretty much all sports. A basketball player wants to bounce the ball fast as they run down the court. That is tough to do with a flat ball. A flatter ball takes a longer time to come back up to the height of your hand. Taking more time to return to your hand results in a slower bounce. You can't run faster than the ball or you'll lose control (and the other team will take the ball away).

Flat tennis balls also get less height when you hit them. They tend to drop faster and not to travel as far. Want to get a shot across the net with a flat ball? You may have to be closer to hit it over. That makes playing the game from the backcourt very difficult. And it also makes you run a lot more.

How are the physics of a flat ball different from those of a bouncy ball? Bouncy balls are measured by their ability to rebound quickly from the surface that they hit. Watch how this works:

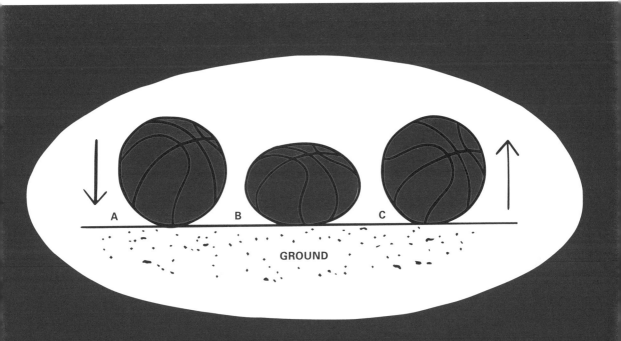

GROUND

Ball A is heading downward with a big force. It may be from your hand or a racket. When Ball B hits the ground, some of the energy is transferred to the ground. The ball deforms slightly and flattens just a tiny bit. As it hits the ground the energy from the ground is reflected back into the ball, so the ball regains its shape and accelerates upward. That gives you Ball C.

A flat ball—one that is not inflated well—will become much more deformed when it's in Ball B's position. Much less energy is transferred to the ground, and thus the energy transferred back to the ball will cause it to accelerate upward more slowly.

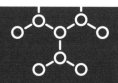

TEST IT OUT

GET A COUPLE of basketballs that you can remove air from. First take a basketball that is very bouncy. Bounce the ball as high as you can. Now take another basketball and let out a little bit of the air. Try bouncing that. Does it go as high? Probably not. That is because it has less rebound energy. What do you learn from this? Make sure that if you're playing a sport that needs a bouncy ball, the ball you're using is inflated well.

But not all sports have round balls. A football is a prolate spheroid. (Bet you didn't know it was called that.) A prolate spheroid is simply an ellipse with two pointy ends. Most people know that a football looks like that.

Footballs didn't always look that way, though. The first football was made out of an inflated pig's bladder. It was much more round.

These round footballs were heavy and difficult to throw. When you did throw them, they didn't travel far at all, they just sort of dropped to the ground. So for the first couple of years of the game, players just tossed the ball to each other using an underhand throw. It wasn't until 1906 that they began using an overhand throw. This resulted in the first forward pass. Still, the football they used weighed one pound, so it was still really heavy. And the round ball did not fly easily through the air.

Finally, in 1920, the football's shape was changed to the one that is still used today. Why the prolate spheroid? Physics. The football's round shape was not designed to reduce drag (the force that slows you down as you move through a fluid). In fact, there was so much drag on the round football, it didn't travel very far at all. Something had to change. The funny part is, like many bits of science, the change most likely came about by accident. One story says that during a game between Princeton University and Rutgers University, the football kept losing air. They stopped several times to blow it back up. But since the ball refused to keep the air, the

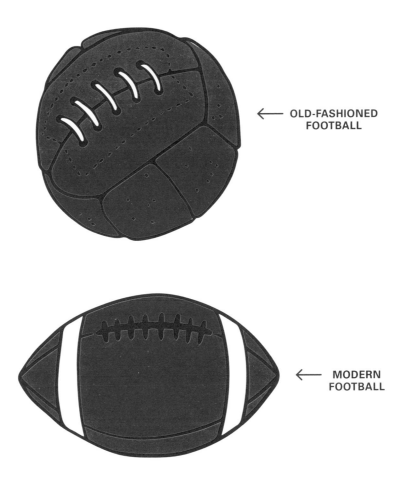

← OLD-FASHIONED FOOTBALL

← MODERN FOOTBALL

teams ended up playing with it even though it was a bit flat. The somewhat flat ball ended up being shaped more like an ellipse. The players realized that this shape made the football easier to grip. That meant they could pass it better and also catch and hold it better. It got them thinking.

Eventually, the shape of the football was changed. It was a good thing, too. Today's football is shaped as a prolate spheroid because it reduces drag and also allows for increased lift. Lift is a force that allows an object to move upward. It acts opposite to gravity. The air gets under the object and lifts it higher. That is why quarterbacks throw their balls higher into the air—to get a greater lift underneath the ball. Lift helps the ball to stay in the air.

SMALLER IS BETTER (FOR SOME SPORTS)

Lift and drag are important forces in all sports. Since each sport has a different focus, the forces needed to act upon the ball are different. For example, baseballs are smaller because they tend to travel very far and very fast. The smaller the object, the smaller the forces acting upon it. A baseball is much smaller than a football and therefore experiences less drag, the force that slows it down. That is why baseballs can travel really fast.

The average speed a major league baseball pitcher throws a baseball between 88 and 92 mph.

Golf balls are tinier than baseballs. That is because they must travel much farther distances than baseballs. A professional golfer may be able to drive their ball as far as 280 yards or more.

Soccer balls, on the other hand, are bigger than either baseballs or golf balls. They are bigger so that people can manage them more easily with their feet and heads. Their bigger size means they have more drag and can't travel as far as either baseballs or golf balls. However, players can put a spin on the ball, which allows them to direct it more easily.

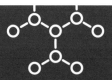

LEARNING ABOUT LIFT AND DRAG

TIME FOR YOU to learn about lift and drag by seeing it in action. Gather all the sports balls you have. Grab a friend if you can. Test each ball for distance by seeing how far you can throw it. Then try kicking each ball. Watch how they fly through the air or roll along the ground. Do they experience lift and drag? You can make a drawing of this to compare each type of ball and the way it moved. By looking at each ball all at once, you may get a feel for how lift and drag work. Knowing about these two forces can definitely help you improve your game as an athlete.

WINDY DAYS

Ever try playing sports on a windy day? What happens to the ball? And to you? Wind increases the drag on everything, and it slows down a ball that has been hit or thrown. It pushes back on you as you run down the field or around the track, or even as you bike up that mountain. With a greater drag force acting on the ball, you will have to put more energy behind that throw. That means pulling your arm back farther and pushing harder as you throw. It means hitting the baseball or tennis ball harder with your bat or racket. It also means running or biking harder to keep going the same speed through the wind.

Is there a way to offset an increased drag caused by wind? Sort of. Most runners will lean into the wind and perhaps hunch their shoulders and drop their head a little. This makes their body a little smaller and allows the drag to lessen. Bikers will hunch way over their bikes, almost bending their bodies in half to reduce wind drag. Football players throw the ball at lower angles to try to reduce the drag on the ball. The idea is that if the football goes through the air at more of a straight line where the point of the ball cuts through the wind, there will be less drag. Does this always work? No. But it can help.

Golfers will keep their shots lower to the ground on windy days. The reason is that the longer the ball is high in the air, the more likely a gust of wind could catch it and throw it off course. But sometimes extra wind can work in your favor. If you are kicking a field goal, you'd rather have the wind behind you. That way it gives your ball an extra push toward the goal. Kicking into the wind is much harder. The wind is basically pushing your ball back toward you, so you'll have to give it an extra bit of energy to make it through those goalposts. Oomph!

FRICTION FUN

Wind is not usually a factor in sports that are played indoors. For example, you'll rarely get a gust of wind while playing hockey or speed skating. However, that doesn't mean drag and friction are any less of an issue. Drag is a concern for speed skaters because, just like a cyclist, the more of their body that is exposed to the air, the greater the drag. Have you ever seen speed skaters? They bend really low and practically curl up on themselves as they skate. That is because they are reducing the drag on their bodies. Drag slows them down and increases their time. Two things you don't want if your goal is to win the race.

Hockey players also bend and duck as they skate. This helps them to go fast. However, they do tend to stand straighter just before they shoot the puck. That is because they want to be able to swing their arm and shoulder back as far as they can before whacking the puck. That gives the puck more energy (and hopefully sends it flying across the ice and into the goal).

Friction on ice is something you probably don't think about. But it is important. Ever wonder why the Zamboni (the ice cleaning machine) goes onto the ice between each quarter during a hockey game? It's to put down a new sheet of ice. This makes the ice smooth again. As the players skate around, their skates cut grooves into the ice. This creates friction and slows the players down. Adding a new layer of ice fills in those grooves so the players can skate much faster.

Every sports field you play on has some level of friction. Most football fields today are made of either natural grass or artificial turf. Grass is something you know. It grows on its own and is cut a certain length for the game. But grass has more friction force than artificial turf. Artificial turf is a man-made surface. It's flatter than grass, which makes it have less friction. But it's also harder, so falling on it does not feel as soft as falling on grass.

Tennis courts can be grass, clay, or hard courts. Grass has a lot of friction and balls don't bounce very well on it. Clay surfaces are made of compressed rock, like shale, stone, or brick. The ball bounces very well on clay because it doesn't have a lot of friction. Hard courts are made of acrylic substance mixed with sand. They are very hard and balls bounce very well. But please don't fall or slide on an acrylic court. It will hurt. Ouch!

Baseball fields are made of dirt and grass. Grass is tough to run on and will also slow down the ball. But the dirt has much less friction and allows balls to travel faster. You can also slide really well in baseball. Be sure to do that safely, though.

Having equipment that is made from the latest technology and engineered with top-of-the-line design can really improve your level of play. How do you design this equipment? That is where math comes in. Yes, you do actually use math in sports, too.

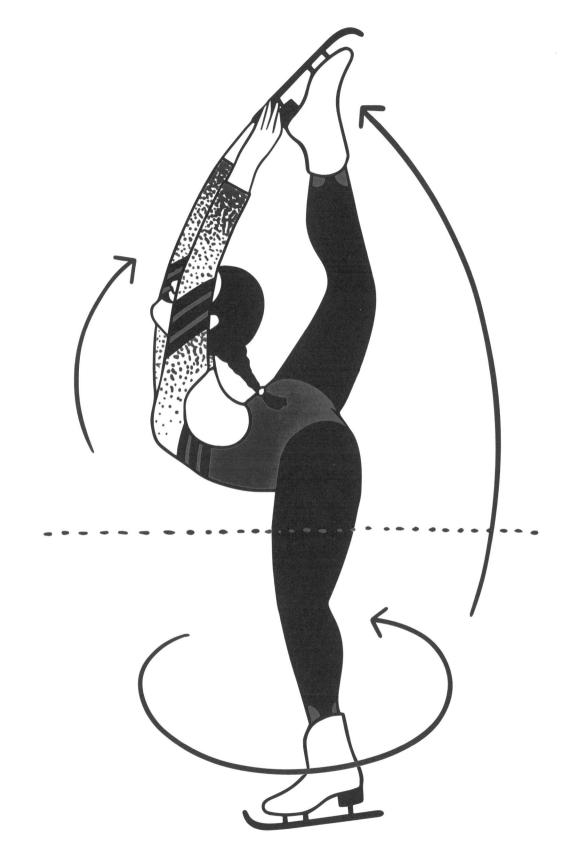

4 MATH + SPORTS = KNOWLEDGE

WHEN YOU THINK of sports, you probably imagine kicking a ball, running a distance, tackling, or even swimming across a pool, but sports also involve a lot of math. That's right. Math! Think about it—don't you keep score in pretty much every sport? Sometimes it is the number of goals you count, but it can also be the time it takes to complete an event. Those all involve numbers, and that means math.

The thing is, people who follow sports really want to know a lot of information. What is the average distance a certain quarterback can throw the ball? How fast does this tennis player usually hit the ball during their serve? Their return? How many times will a team win if they are up by five or more points? Come on. Admit it. You know some of the answers to those questions, don't you? Or maybe even different ones. Those answers are referred to as statistics. Statistics is the science of collecting numerical data, analyzing that data, and comparing it to other numbers. (Hint: It is what the sports announcers talk about while you are watching a sporting event.) If you follow sports regularly, chances are you know a lot of statistics about your favorite team and players.

Finally, math is also used to calculate probability. Probability tells you the number of times something is likely to happen. In the last chapter you learned how to shoot a basketball correctly. What if you want to know the chances that you will make the shot if you stand in a certain place on the court? Probability will help you with that. Statistics and probability go together when you are analyzing sporting competitions, and the players, too. It is used by coaches, recruiters, and even players themselves to see how they are progressing. Sports would have no winners if you didn't keep score. Now you know why math is so important!

SCORING THE GAME

You have just been named the team's statistician. Great! What does that mean? And how do you do your job? It means that you are in charge of creating and maintaining all the statistics, or stats, for the team and probably for each player, too. Sounds like a big task. It is. But you are up to it. You just need to know a few things to get you started. First of all, how many points do you earn for each score? It depends. What game are you playing? And is it a team sport or individual sport? (It matters.)

Each game has its own set of scores. Let's take a look at some of the most familiar team sports. (Note: This does not include a list of ALL sports. If you have questions about a sport not listed, go look it up!)

TEAM SPORT	SCORING
BASEBALL	1 point for each time a player crosses home plate (before reaching the 3rd out).
HOCKEY	1 point for the puck crossing the line into the net. Point goes to the team who does not own the net.
SOCCER, LACROSSE, FIELD HOCKEY, RUGBY	1 point for the ball crossing the goal line into the net. Point goes to the team who does not own the net.
BASKETBALL	1 point for getting the ball into the net from a free throw line (as a result of a foul being called). 2 points for getting the ball into the basket while shooting within the 3-point-line circle on the court. 3 points for getting the ball into the basket while shooting behind the 3-point-line circle on the court.
FOOTBALL	6 points for a touchdown (when the player holding the ball crosses the goal line of the other team). 1 point for an extra point as the ball is kicked through the uprights after a touchdown has been made. 3 points for a field goal (when the ball is kicked through the uprights). 2 points for a safety (when the ball carrier is tackled in his own end zone OR when the ball is considered to be out of play in the defenders' end zone and they are responsible for it happening).

INDIVIDUAL SPORT*	SCORING
TENNIS	To win a game, you must get 4 points. But the points are counted as 15, 30, 40, game. You win a point when your ball is not successfully returned by your opponent. To win a match, you must win between 2 and 3 sets. Each set consists of at least 6 games.
SWIMMING, RUNNING, BIKING	Each of the events are timed, and the competitor with the lowest time wins.

* Note: These can also be played as a team. In that case, the team usually gets the overall score/time.

BASKETBALL COURT

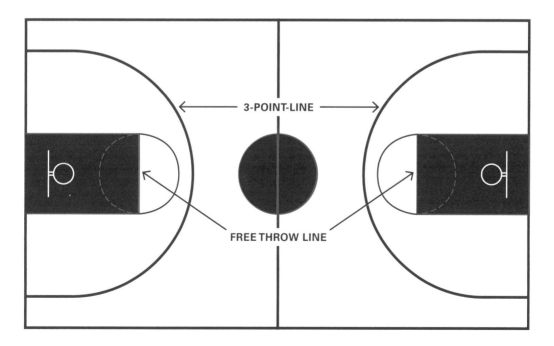

Did you get all that? Scoring in some games is much more complicated than scoring in others. It's not difficult to do, though, once you understand it. The next step for a statistician is to calculate some statistics. Are you ready to give it a try?

CALCULATING TIMES

You are in charge of creating the stats for the swim team. The coach wants to know the four best swimmers to put on a relay. This one is pretty easy. You just have to collect the times that have been recorded for each swimmer for that event.

For the 400-meter relay, each swimmer will swim 100 meters of freestyle. Since you have been recording all the times for each swimmer who competed in the individual 100-meter freestyle swim, you can figure this out. Just pick the four swimmers with the lowest times.

So if you were to pick the swimmers with the best time to put into the 4×100 relay, you would need to pick swimmers A, B, D, and F.

What if you were asked to pick the best swimmers to make up the 400m medley relay? In the medley relay, one swimmer swims 100m backstroke, another person swims 100m butterfly, a third the 100m breaststroke, and the fourth the 100m freestyle. For that you need to take a good look at the statistics.

Swimmer D is fastest in the freestyle, but also is the second fastest in the butterfly. Swimmer F is the fastest in both the backstroke and the butterfly. Swimmer B is the fastest in the breaststroke. This is where the statistics are helpful for the coach. They can take a look at the times to help them decide. But ultimately, it also comes down to what the swimmer wants and what the coach thinks is best for the team. What would you choose?

How about swimmer B for breaststroke because they are the fastest in that. Swimmer D for the freestyle. Swimmer F for backstroke, because that is the lead-off swim and will get you ahead the fastest. That leaves Swimmer A for the butterfly. This looks like a good choice. Is it the one you'd make? Perhaps not. But using statistics can help you make an informed choice.

This plan also works for runners in track and for cycling, since both of those sports are based on individual times and team times.

	SWIMMER					
	A	**B**	**C**	**D**	**E**	**F**
100 M FREESTYLE (IN MIN:SECONDS)	0:58.5	0:58.9	0:60.1	0:57.9	0:59.0	0:58.4
100 M BACKSTROKE (IN MIN:SECONDS)	1:07	1:06	1:05	1:05.2	1:08	1:04.8
100 M BREASTSTROKE (IN MIN:SECONDS)	1:15.0	1:14.8	1:15.3	1:17.1	1:16.7	1:15.6
100 M BUTTERFLY (IN MIN:SECONDS)	1:00.5	1:01.3	1:01.8	1:00.3	1:02.1	0:59

TAKING A SPLIT TIME OF A RELAY

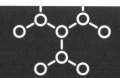

SOMETIMES YOU NEED to record the times of each member of a relay team while they are actually performing. If you have multiple watches you can do this easily. Just start the time on each watch from zero when the next individual relay team member takes off. If you have only one watch,

then you will need to record the times as splits. A split time measures the time each individual athlete performs, but does not stop the overall time on the watch. Punch the split button each time one athlete ends their leg of the relay and the next one begins their portion. After the event is over, write down each athlete's time.

What you will have is the overall time, which is the time for all four athletes combined. Why do you care about this? Coaches and statisticians keep track of split times. They use them to compare to other athletes. It tells them who is the fastest, but also in which place the athlete performs the best. Sometimes an athlete is a great starter. Sometimes they are better at finishing. And there are athletes that excel in the middle of a relay. You may notice that the splits are slightly different. That is not just because the athletes are faster or slower than each other; in a relay you may cover different distances. For example, if you are the starter in a running relay, you have to start from scratch and you run only to the beginning of the relay lane. The second runner runs all of the relay lane and then into the next, so they may be running just a few yards longer than the rest of the team. The same for the third runner. The last runner has the shortest route, running a few yards less than everyone else.

To take a split: Many watches have a split button. (Check to see if yours does.) How does it work? When the first athlete takes off (swimming, biking, running, etc.), you start the time. As the first athlete reaches the point where the next athlete is ready to go, push the split button on your watch.

Those calculations didn't seem too difficult, did they? It was relatively easy to calculate and compare those statistics. Now things are going to get a bit more complicated.

SOCCER STATS

Soccer statistics are kept on each player and for the team, too. This allows the coaches to compare players and put in the ones who will perform the best. Statistics also let the coach know which player is best suited to a certain position.

Some of the soccer statistics that are kept (both for overall and per game) include:

- Goals: when the player scores a goal

- Assists: when one player passes to another player who then scores

- Shots: how many times the player shoots the ball to try to make a goal

- Shot percentage on goal: the amount of times the player shoots the ball divided by the number of goals they made

- Minutes played: how many minutes each team member plays in the game

- Fouls: how many fouls they receive (yellow card and red card)

For the goalie, a few other statistics are kept:

- Saves: how many times they prevent the ball from going into the goal

- Goals on goalie: how many goals are scored on them

There are also statistics on the number of times a player touches a ball, the number of times a player passes a ball, the amount of time they have the ball, and so much more. It just depends on how much time you have to record all these statistics. And the time you have to go through them all.

BASKETBALL STATS
Basketball, like most sports, keeps statistics on both the team and the player. The important information to know about a team includes:

- Points per game: the total points a team earns for that game

- Rebounds per game: the number of times a player recovers a ball after it has been shot at the basket but doesn't go in

- Assists per game: the number of times one player helps another out when making a basket

- Blocks per game: the number of times a player successfully blocks another player's shot, preventing a basket

- Steals per game: the number of times one player steals the ball from another

- Field goal percentage per game: the total number of

baskets made divided by the number of shots taken during the game

- Three-pointers made per game: the total number of three-point shots (taken from behind the three-point line) in one game

- Three-point percentage: the total number of three-point baskets made divided by the number of them taken

- Free throws made per game: the total number of free throws made by each team during the game

Those same stats are kept for individual players, too. That way the coach can see how each player is performing. Of course, these statistics are tracked by many other people, too. Sports announcers, fans, and, yes, even other teams. People love to use these stats to talk to each other about their favorite players and teams. Who is your favorite player? Do you know their stats? It wouldn't be surprising if you did. Avid sports fans often keep up-to-date on all these statistics.

FOOTBALL STATS

Football keeps statistics about all aspects of the game. Just to name a few—how many yards a player runs (rushing), how many yards a ball travels in a pass, how often the quarterback throws a completion or an interception, and, of course, how many times the field goal kicker makes the field goal. Let's take a look at some of the major statistics that people track in football:

- Number of games played

- Total points

- Points per game: total points divided by number of games

- Rushing yards: the number of yards a player gets while holding the ball before being tackled

- Rushing yards per game: total rushing yards divided by number of games

- Passing yards—the number of yards the ball travels while in the air from the quarterback to the receiver

- Passing yards per game: total passing yards divided by number of games

HOW WELL IS THE QUARTERBACK DOING?

WHEN YOU THINK of a football team, what person on the team do you usually think of first? Probably the quarterback. He is typically the most visible member. After all, he is the one who is involved in all the offensive plays—that's when the team has the ball and is trying to score. In fact, the quarterback is the person who actually controls the play. They throw passes, make handoffs to runners, and even toss the ball to others to throw. It is important for a team to have a good quarterback. Naturally, that means there are statistics that apply just to the quarterback. This helps coaches to understand how well the quarterback is playing. Quarterbacks are also given a rating based on these stats.

Sample stats for an NFL quarterback might be:

ATT	534	Att: Attempt, or how many times the quarterback threw the football
COMP	365	Comp: Completions, or how many times the ball was thrown and caught
PCT COMP	68.4	Pct Comp: Percent Completions = number of completions divided by number of attempts
YDS	4,985	Yds: Yardage = the amount of yards that the receiver ran once he caught the ball

YDS/ATT	9.3	Yds/Att: Yards per Attempt = the average number of yards the receiver ran each time he caught the ball
TD	32	TD: Touchdowns = the number of touchdowns the quarterback has earned (either by throwing or running)
INT	16	Int: Interceptions = the number of times the quarterback threw the ball and it was caught by the other team
RATING	103.2	Rating: Passer rating = used to analyze the quarterback's performance

Calculating the Passer rating is pretty complicated. The best way to start is to break it down into four different formulas, then combine them all at the end.

FORMULA 1

Completions divided by Attempts = Total #1
Take Total #1 and subtract 0.30 to get Total #2
Take Total #2 and multiply by 5

Example (using the numbers from the chart above):
Formula 1 = 365 ÷ 534 = 0.68
0.68 − 0.30 = 0.38
0.38 × 5 = 1.90

(text continues on page 140)

FORMULA 2

Passing yards divided by Attempts = Total #3
Take Total #3 and subtract 3 to get Total #4
Take Total #4 and multiply by 0.25

Example:
Formula 2 = 4985 ÷ 534 = 9.34
9.34 − 3 = 6.34
6.34 × 0.25 = 1.59

FORMULA 3

Touchdowns divided by Attempts = Total #5
Take Total #5 and multiply the result by 20

Example:
Formula 3 = 32 ÷ 534 = 0.06
0.06 × 20 = 1.20

FORMULA 4

Interceptions divided by Attempts = Total #6
Take Total #6 multiplied by 25 to get Total #7
Take 2.375 and subtract Total #7 to get Total #8

Example:
Formula 4 = 16 ÷ 534 = 0.03
0.03 x 25 = 0.75
2.375 − 0.75 = 1.63

PASSER RATING

Formula 1 + Formula 2 + Formula 3 + Formula 4 = Total #9
Take Total #9 and divide by 6 to get Total #10
Take Total #10 and multiply by 100 to get the Passer rating

Example:
1.90 + 1.59 + 1.20 + 1.63 = 6.32
6.32 ÷ 6 = 1.05
1.05 x 100 = 105

A rating of 100 or more is a great rating for a quarterback. An average quarterback has a rating between 80 and 100. If the passer rating is less than 80, that means the quarterback may not be performing very well.

BASEBALL STATS

Some sports keep track of A LOT of statistics. Baseball, for example, has nine basic statistics that they keep compiled on each player. But there are actually a lot more statistics that baseball fans love to watch. Not all of them are listed here (that would take too much space). If you're interested, just do an internet search on "baseball stats" and you will find a ton of numbers to keep you happy. You'll get enough information to have a long conversation with any other devoted baseball fan.

Now that you have a chance to see the statistics, there are a few definitions you should know (just to make it easy for those who don't follow baseball):

- Strikeout (K): when the player swings the bat three times without hitting the ball during one time at bat.

- Base on Balls, or Walk (BB): when the player does not hit four balls that are each thrown out of the strike zone. The umpire then tells the player to go to first base.

- Error (E): a mistake made by a ballplayer that allows the opposing team's player to continue an at bat or to advance to the next base.

HITTERS	AB	R	H	RBI	BB	K
PLAYER 1 3B	4	1	1	0	0	1
PLAYER 2 RF	4	1	1	1	0	1
PLAYER 3 2B	3	0	0	0	0	1
PLAYER 4 C	1	0	0	0	1	0
PLAYER 5 DH	3	0	0	0	0	1

- Put Out (PO): when a fielder catches a fly ball; catches a thrown ball, which puts out the runner; or tags a runner while he is off the base. The runner is considered to be out and must leave the field and go back to the dugout. Each team gets three outs per inning.

- Fielder's Choice (FC): when a batter gets to first base because the opposing team chose to put another player out.

- Sacrifice Play (SH): when the batter deliberately gets out to advance his teammate who is on another base.

- At Bat (AB): when the player takes a turn at batting, which results in either a hit, a strike-out, an error, or a fielder's choice. What doesn't count as an at bat is: a base on balls, a sacrifice play, or if the batter is hit by the ball. This stat indicates the number of times the player comes to the plate in a game.

- Runs (R): when the player crosses home plate to score.

- Runs Batted In (RBI): when the player hits the ball and other teammates run in and cross home plate to score.

- Hit (H): when the batter hits the ball and takes a base as a result.

These numbers are all just counted. For example, as each player gets another run, the run total goes up. This happens for all of those numbers.

The next three stats are recorded to help understand how well the player performs when they bat.

- Batting average (AVG or BA)—you calculate this by taking the player's total hits (H) and dividing them by the total number of at bats (AB). This is calculated per season, not by game. That makes it easier to compare players because one might have a great game and a high AVG, while another one does not.

  Player #2 has had 1 hit for 4 at bats this season. You would calculate his AVG this way:

  1 ÷ 4 = 0.25

- On Base Percentage (OBP): this tells you how often a player gets on base. This includes getting a hit, a walk, or hit by a pitch. It does not include errors and fielder's choice. For some baseball clubs, a player's OBP is more important than his batting average. This tells the coach how much they can count on this player always getting on base. That is a good thing, because the more times you get on base, the more likely you are to score.

To calculate OBP, you add the total number of hits (H), walks (BB), and hit-by-pitch, and divide the sum by the number of at bats (AB), walks (BB), hit-by-pitches (HBP), and sacrifice flies (SF).

OBP = (H + BB + HBP) ÷ (AB + BB + HBP + SF)

How is this used by teams? They take the average OBP for the entire league and then compare their players to it. The average OBP changes each year, but it typically runs around .300 to .325.

Statisticians know that OBP is about 60 points higher than the batting average (BA), so that puts the batting average for the whole league around .240 to .265. That is pretty standard. As long as your individual OBP is near or around the league OBP average, you are good.

- Slugging (SLG): This gives you a look at what type of hits the player has, and how many bases they get out of their hits.

1B = FIRST BASE

2B = SECOND BASE

3B = THIRD BASE

HR = HOME RUN

You take the number of hits that resulted in getting to each base, add them together and divide by the total at bats (AB).

WHAT IS A GOOD BATTING AVERAGE?

HOW DO YOU know if your batting average is good or not? Typically, the minimum batting average that most major league players want to get is around .250. To be considered as a good hitter in MLB (Major League Baseball) you need to have a .300 average. If you want to be an excellent hitter, you will have an AVG of around .350. Anything higher than that is phenomenal.

Here is the calculation:

**SLG =
(1B + (2 X 2B) + (3X 3B) +
(4 X HR)
ALL DIVIDED BY AB**

What's a good SLG? Something close to .350 is considered to be pretty good, especially when combined with an OBP of .400. An SLG of .450 is really good, and an SLG of .550 is excellent!

The stats you see here are mostly to tell you how an individual player is doing offensively, or when they are batting. There are a whole different set of stats to look at to see how they are playing while they are in the field. And the pitchers? They have their own stats, too. Baseball is a sport that lends itself to A LOT of math!

PERCENTAGES AND PROBABILITY IN SPORTS

Sports fans love talking about percentages. Want to know the percentage of wins vs. losses for the team, the coach, the individual athlete? That can be calculated. What is the chance that a basketball player makes a shot from the different areas of the court? You can determine that, too. Want to know the probability of your team making the playoffs? There is a calculation for that. Many of these calculations are complicated and require up-to-the-minute data. That means you must keep track of your team throughout the season to be able to predict where they will finish.

Probability is a chance that something will happen. Do probability calculations come true? Sometimes, yes. And sometimes, no. The thing about probability is that it doesn't always take into account the human factor. Teams that are ranked low and seem to have no chance can have a really great game and beat a big rival. That changes everything.

Still, if you follow sports, it's good to have an idea of what percentages and probabilities people are tracking—if for no other reason than to have a great conversation about it.

WINNING OR LOSING?

Sometimes you just want to know quickly how a team is doing. The easiest thing to calculate is their win-loss percentage. For that you take the total number of games they won and divide it by the total number of games they played. You can do this for each season, or for the entire time the team has been around. The win-loss percentage is usually calculated for each coach with the team. That way coaches can be compared to each other.

WIN-LOSS PERCENTAGE = TOTAL NUMBER OF WINS × 100 = TOTAL NUMBER OF GAMES PLAYED

If a team plays 80 games a year and wins 55 of them, their win-loss percentage is calculated this way: $55 \div 80 = 0.69 \times 100 = 69$ percent.

That is a decent number, since the games won are more than 50 percent. If you want to be considered a good winning team, then your percentage should be more than 65 to 70 percent. Anything higher than that is great! The same goes for a coach.

A coach's win-loss percentage is pretty important. If they have a high one, that means they may continue to get contracts to stay, which could also result in a pay raise. A low win-loss percentage? That can mean that they won't be with that team for very long.

BEST PLACE TO SHOOT A BASKET (AND SCORE)

Do you play basketball? If so, you know that whether or not you make a basket depends on many things, one of which is where you are located on the court. You may think that this is a standard thing, that the shot percentages for everyone in a certain place on the court are the same. They aren't. Interestingly enough, the shots closer to the basket but made from the side are more difficult for some players than others. Field goal percentages

NBA FIELD GOAL PERCENTAGE

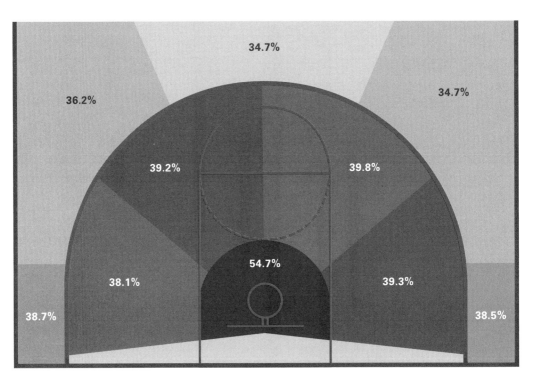

can be determined by team and player. Each one of them can be different. A team in the NBA (National Basketball Association) may include up to fifteen players. The shot percentage picture for the whole team is going to look a lot different from an image of just one player. Why? Each player has a collection of shots that they are good at, ones that they make a large amount of the time. Maybe they are great at slam dunks, or a really awesome three-point shooter. Their shooting percentage will reflect that.

Here is a sample of a percent shot average image for the entire NBA.

The basketball hoop is located at the bottom of the image. The area around the hoop, naturally, has the highest percentage of baskets made. Why? Ever watch a basketball game? The players typically move toward the basket to get closer to shoot. You notice that as you get farther out

INDIVIDUAL FIELD GOAL PERCENTAGE

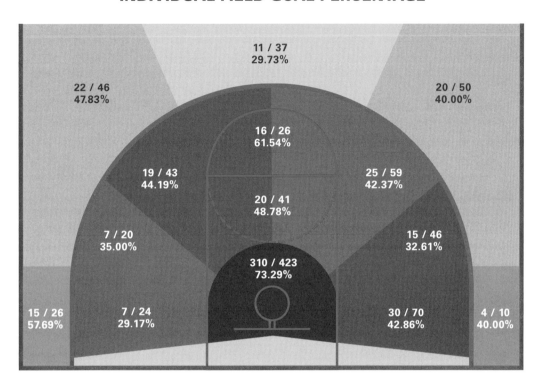

from that initial area, the percent of baskets that are made drops significantly. Still, it is pretty similar in that they are all around 34 to 39 percent. That means that slightly more than one out of every three shots taken in those areas goes in. Not bad. Can you say that about your basketball game?

Now let's see what an individual player's stats might look like:

On this image you will see two numbers, like this: 310/423. That means that the player made 310 baskets out of the 423 shots they took in that area near the basket. By dividing 310 into 423, you get 73.29 percent—which is the number below the fraction.

This player appears to be really good at shooting the ball by the basket and from the top of the round circle (known as the key). But this player isn't so great at certain areas. This information is very valuable to a coach. It allows the coach to help the player play to their strengths, which is to say that when she is in an area where she makes most of her shots, she should get the ball.

This diagram also tells you where the player prefers to be when she shoots the ball. How can you see that? Look at the number of times this player has taken a shot from the different areas. There are almost three times as many shots from the right side of the basket as there are from the left side of the basket.

That is great information for the coach, but also for the other team. If you were on the other team, wouldn't that be interesting information to have? Think about it. If you knew that this player loved to go to the right side to shoot, then you'd put your best defensive player on her to prevent the shot. Forcing the player to go to the other side of the basket means she has a smaller probability of making that shot. Games have been won using this strategy.

CALCULATING TRUE SHOOTING PERCENTAGE PER PLAYER

Coaches like to know how efficient each player is when they shoot, meaning how many times they shoot and score. To do that, they calculate the player's true shooting percentage. Like most statistics, this is a little complicated.

Step 1: Decide how many games you want to use in your calculation. A quarter of the season? A half? The whole season?

Step 2: Take the number of free throws attempted (but not necessarily made) and multiply it by 0.44.

Step 3: Take the answer from step 2 and add it to the number of field goals attempted (but not necessarily made).

Step 4: Take the answer from step 3 and multiply it by 2.

Step 5: Take the total points made and divide it by the answer to step 4.

Field Goals Made (FGM) = 2818	Free Throws Made (FTM) = 754
Field Goals Attempted (FGA) = 1909	Free Throws Attempted (FTA) = 858

Did you get all that? No? Okay, let's do an example.

Here are the stats of Player A for the entire season:

Step 1: This will be for the entire season.

Step 2: FTA × 0.44 = 858 × 0.44 = 377.52

Step 3: 377.52 + FGA = 377.52 + 1909 = 2286.52

Step 4: 2286.52 × 2 = 4573.04

Step 5: 2818 ÷ 4573.04 = 0.62

ANOTHER WAY TO CALCULATE TRUE SHOOTING PERCENTAGE

DO YOU HAVE a favorite player in the NBA or WNBA? Then you probably want to know what their shooting percentage is. You can use the calculations above to figure it out yourself, or you can do an internet search on your player and look up their stats. If you want to compare that player to others, search on "NBA Stats and Leaders," and you'll get to see how all the top players are performing.

THREE-POINT SHOT PERCENTAGE

The three-point shot is a great way to add fast points to your score. Many players are becoming much better at shooting from behind the three-point line. Why do you get more points for this shot than for a regular one? It's supposed to be much more difficult to shoot from this distance. It takes great skill to find the right angle, give the ball the maximum push, and then aim it at the basket from this area of the court. Players that can do this are rewarded with an extra point for their efforts.

Teams have figured out that if they have a few players who are consistently making baskets from behind the three-point line, they can really run up their score quickly. Therefore, coaches are keeping track of the statistics of players who shoot from behind the three-point line.

Calculating the three-point shot percentage is easy. To calculate an individual player's three-point shot percentage, just take the total number of three-point baskets made, divide by the total shots taken per game, and multiply the result by 100.

3-POINT SHOT % = NUMBER OF 3-POINT BASKETS MADE PER GAME ÷ NUMBER OF TOTAL SHOTS TAKEN PER GAME × 100

If Player S takes 45 shots in one game and makes 15 field goals and 10 three-point shots, what is his three-point shot percentage?

3-POINT SHOT % = (10 ÷ 45) × 100 = 22.2%

The three-point shot percentage average for the NBA is 36 percent. Anything higher than that is considered to be excellent. If a whole team can have a three-point shot percentage of 38 percent, that is an indicator that they may be on their way to the playoffs. Now you know how important it is to have good three-point shooters on your team. No wonder coaches and statisticians keep track of this percentage.

CHANCES OF HITTING A HOME RUN

Baseball fans keep so many different statistics, it's hard to keep track of them all. Here's one that you may find useful yourself (well, if you're a baseball player): What are your chances of hitting a home run? There are so many things to consider. First of all, the field where you are playing. How far is the distance to the back fence? In order for it to be a home run, the ball has to go over the fence. So the distance you have to hit the ball is definitely a factor. Next is the direction you hit the ball. That can include the speed, angle, and actual direction that you are hitting the ball. Does your ball go high and straight? Curve low and to the left? All of those things play into this probability.

To make things easy, though, you can just count up the number of home runs you have hit this season and divide by the number of pitches you have seen while at the plate, then multiply the result by 100.

Example: Player T has seen 1,864 pitches this season and has 25 home runs. What is the chance that he hits a home run?

$$(25 \div 1864) \times 100 = 1.3\%$$

BASICALLY, PLAYER T HITS A HOME RUN IN ABOUT 1.3 OUT OF EVERY 100 PITCHES.

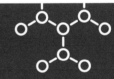

SWINGING FOR THE FENCES

HAVE YOU HEARD the term "swinging for the fences"? It's an old saying that meant the batter was trying to hit a home run by swinging the bat so hard the ball went over the back fence. While the saying may be outdated, the idea isn't. Many baseball players dream of hitting a home run. Some

(text continues on page 152)

do more than others. Clearly, looking at the probability calculations above, hitting a home run is not easy. Is there anything you can do to help with your chances? Sure.

Follow these steps and it will up your odds (chances) of hitting one.

- Use a composite bat if you can (not a wooden one). These provide a harder hit to the ball.
- Swing as fast as possible OR use a heavy bat.
- Baseball fields where the temperature is very hot and humid help to carry the ball farther. Bonus if it's also at high altitude, where the air is thinner and the ball stays up longer.
- Some baseball stadiums have fences that are farther away from home plate than others. You'll have a better chance of hitting a home run if you're in a stadium that has a fence closer to home plate.
- Hit the ball in the sweet spot of your bat.
- Hit it at an angle of between 25 and 30 degrees. That gives the ball enough lift and is the best angle to get the longest distance.

Oh, yes, and practice helps (of course)! Give it a shot next time you're up at bat. See if you can really swing for the fences and make it.

PITCHER RATING—EARNED RUN AVERAGE

Just as a football coach wants to know how their quarterback is performing, the coach of a baseball team needs a way to check on their pitcher. After all, the way the pitcher is playing has a huge impact on the game. If they get a lot of strikeouts, there is less chance for the other team to score. If the pitcher has a lot of base hits or home runs hit off him, well, then that leads to big scores...for the other team. Not exactly what a coach wants.

How do you check on the pitcher's performance? A calculation called the earned run average (ERA) can tell you. The ERA is the number of earned runs a pitcher has in each inning. (Remember, each full game has nine innings.) Why do they use the term *earned run*? An earned run average does not count any scores that may have happened because of an error or a passed ball (a pitch that the catcher drops).

To calculate the ERA, you need to know three things:

- The number of innings the pitcher played

- The number of runs scored per inning

- The total number of innings

Here is the calculation:

ERA = (EARNED RUNS × TOTAL INNINGS) ÷ INNINGS PITCHED

Example: Player Z pitches for six innings, during which eight runs are earned. The game went to all nine innings.

What do you know?

Innings pitcher played = 6

Earned runs = 8

Total innings played = 9

ERA = (8 × 9) ÷ 6 = 12

THINGS TO NOTE ABOUT CALCULATING ERA

ERA IS BASED on a normal game with 9 innings, so the total innings played is always 9.

Do NOT count errors or passed balls.

If one run scores on an error and there are players on the other bases, when they score they are unearned runs and do not count toward a pitcher's ERA.

What is a good ERA?

3–4 is very good

4–5 is average for MLB pitchers

5+ is below average

This is an ERA calculation for just one game. ERA is normally calculated over a whole season. It is possible to have a bad game where you give up a lot of runs as a pitcher. But if Player Z continues to have an ERA that is this high, he may end up moving to a new position on the field.

As you can probably guess (get it—guess? probability?), there are so many different probability and percentage statistics that are being tracked. Imagine stats for *every* sport! That's right. Somewhere out there is a person who knows the statistics of a football game that happened twenty years ago or the chances that an athlete can hit a homer in a baseball stadium that was torn down years ago.

It's fun to keep track of sports statistics. Some people even use statistics to "build" their own teams and have them "play" against each other. What does that mean? Have you ever heard of fantasy sports teams? They have a pretty big following and can be fun to play. For FUN, not betting.

WHAT ARE FANTASY SPORTS?

Fantasy sports have made-up teams created by the fans of a particular sport. For example, say you want to have a fantasy football team with your friends. Each of you creates your own team (and team name!) and then you draft players, just like the real NFL does. The key to this process is that you can pick players from any team to be on your team. That's right. You can have a quarterback from one team and a running back from another team. It doesn't matter. The only rule is that you are allowed a certain number of players and no more.

How does your team "play"? You track the statistics of each player as they play in real-life games. Each player earns points for their performance. You add up the points all of your players get for your team that week. If your team has more points than your friends' teams, you win that week. There are tons of stats that you can track with your fantasy football team. Most of them are split up into team stats, player stats, and position stats (running back, receiver, etc.).

If you love numbers and statistics, fantasy sports is for you. Again, just for FUN and not for betting. But hey, it's having fun with sports and math. It doesn't get any better than that.

CALCULATING THE PERFECT SPIN OR FLIP

Statistics and probability are the two main things you think of when you think of math and sports, but there are other ways to combine the two. Did you ever wonder how gymnasts and skaters do those amazing multiple flips? How they can fly into the air and do two, three, or four turns? How do they know that is even possible? Math.

TRIPLE AXEL TRIUMPH

One of the biggest and perhaps most beautiful jumps in figure skating is the triple axel. Have you ever seen it? It's amazing. The skater must build speed, push off the outside edge of the skate on one foot, propel themselves into the air, spin around three and a half times, and land on the outside edge of the opposite skate backward. Sounds easy, right? It's not. As of 2018, only eight women have successfully completed a triple axel during a competition.

Why is a triple axel so difficult? It takes a huge amount of power and precision to land one. Let's take a look at the physics and the math involved.

The calculations to determine how to do the triple axel are really complicated. Coaches usually take videos of the skater and then analyze the biomechanics (or how their body works). But in general, the initial jump must be high enough for them to complete three and a half rotations (turns) before they land. The big force that they are competing against? Gravity. As you've learned before, as soon as an object goes into the air, gravity acts to pull it down again.

To begin the skater needs to generate a lot of speed. That is why you'll see them skate around the rink for a little bit. They are gathering their horizontal speed. Then *whoosh!* They jump as high as they can, hoping that their speed can reach about 4.8 meters per second. This is 14 percent higher velocity than if the skater is doing only a single axel. Why so fast? The speed helps to drive the skater higher into the air. Part of this is accomplished when they pull up their leg for the extra push.

Once they get into the air, they pull everything in tightly. Their arms are against their chest and their legs are intertwined. The idea is to make themselves as small as possible so that they can spin very fast. If their body is stretched out too much, they will spin at a slower rate. Which means they won't be able to complete all three and a half rotations before landing on the ice again.

As the skate comes out of the last half turn, they must land on their opposite foot. The entire force of their body goes into their foot, which is about eight to ten times that of the skater's own body weight. Oomph! That is a lot of force. And yet skaters do these amazing jumps and make it look so easy and graceful.

PREPARATION

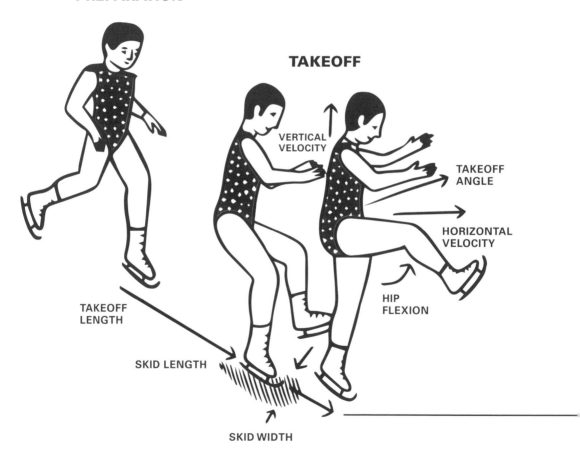

TAKEOFF

VERTICAL VELOCITY

TAKEOFF ANGLE

HORIZONTAL VELOCITY

HIP FLEXION

TAKEOFF LENGTH

SKID LENGTH

SKID WIDTH

Are the skaters actually thinking about the physics and the math when they do the jumps? No. They are concentrating on maintaining their form. They are keeping their heads up, their arms tight to their chest, and their legs crossed, and then at the right moment they land. To do this jump well, skaters will practice it over and over again. They are training their bodies and their brains to know how it feels to perform the jump properly. It is a long and difficult road to master a jump like this, but totally worth it in the end if you can land it properly in a competition.

FLIGHT

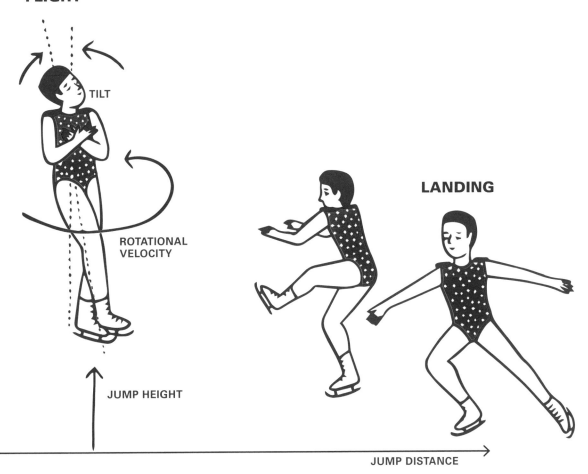

TILT

ROTATIONAL VELOCITY

LANDING

JUMP HEIGHT

JUMP DISTANCE

GYMNAST FLIPS, TWISTS, AND TURNS

If you like to watch gymnastics, then you've seen the amazing flips, twists, and turns gymnasts do during their performances. They are literally flying through the air and landing gracefully at the end. The floor exercise is where the most spectacular flips take place. First of all, the floor is composed of springs that give gymnasts a little extra bounce, and it also cushions their landing. But the floor alone is not responsible for the incredible height and number of twists and flips a gymnast can do.

Simone Biles, one of the most famous gymnasts of her time, has created her own flip. It's called the triple-double. That means that she does a double backflip with three twists. Can't imagine that? It's tough to think about but wonderful to watch. If we were to do the calculations on Simone's flip, it would look something like this:

Moment of inertia is the time where the body starts its movement. Each movement has its own moment of inertia. *Rotational acceleration* is the speed at which she is rotating. *Torque* is the measurement of the force that causes an object to rotate.

As you can see, this is pretty complicated. Simone jumps almost ten feet into the air to complete this trick. For someone who is only four feet eight inches, that is a feat in and of itself. Simone jumps really hard into the floor and uses the springs to propel her like a rocket into the air, all the while executing these flips and turns with precision. She keeps her body tightly curled to maintain her speed, and then lands perfectly on the ground. An awesome sight to see!

Hopefully, after reading this chapter you realize that math is very important in sports. It is used to keep track of player and team performance, to keep scores, and even to help athletes achieve amazing feats in physics. It's kind of important that you pay attention in math class now, don't you think?

Sports and sports science are a huge part of society. Tens of thousands of people watch sports, play

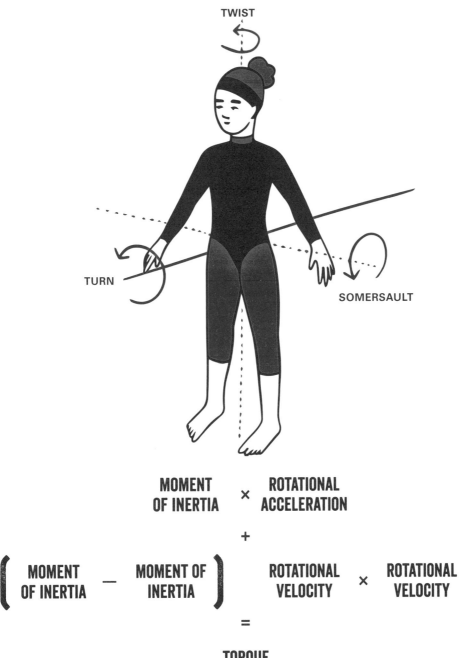

TWIST

TURN

SOMERSAULT

MOMENT
OF INERTIA $\times$ ROTATIONAL
ACCELERATION

+

(MOMENT
OF INERTIA $-$ MOMENT OF
INERTIA) ROTATIONAL
VELOCITY $\times$ ROTATIONAL
VELOCITY

=

TORQUE

sports, and talk about sports. Want to make friends? Sports is a good way to do so. People with all kinds of skills are needed. You can get on a team and be a player, a coach, or even the statistician. Each person is an important part of the overall team. The idea that sports and science are completely unrelated is simply not true. Without physics, brain science, math, and engineering skills, there wouldn't be any sports.

How could you design a really great tennis racket or golf club without understanding the forces and motion? You need to know about materials and body mechanics (how you move), too. Science and sports are forever intertwined, as they should be. Think about that the next time you are running across the field to get to practice. How can science help you at your sporting event today? Grab this book and find out. You'll be glad you did, and who knows? You may just learn something you didn't know…a secret about the science of sports.

BIBLIOGRAPHY

Aceves, Ana. "Wearable Technology May Help Make Football Safer." *PBS*, February 3, 2018. https://www.pbs.org/wgbh/nova/article/wearable-technology-may-help-make-football-safer/.

American Chemical Society. "Video: How Silver Nanoparticles Cut Odors." Phys.org, September 20, 2018. https://phys.org/news/2018-09-video-silver-nanoparticles-odors.html.

"The Average Height of NBA Players—from Point Guards to Centers." The Hoops Geek, December 15, 2018. https://www.thehoopsgeek.com/average-nba-height/.

Bannon, Tim. "Balance Beam: The Most Treacherous—and Mesmerizing—10 Centimeters in Sports." *Chicago Tribune*, August 7, 2016. https://www.chicagotribune.com/sports/olympics/ct-balance-beam-olympic-gymnastics-spt-0808-20160807-story.html.

"Baseball Swing, Blink of an Eye or Google Search: What's Quicker?" Diamond Kinetics, April 14, 2015. https://diamondkinetics.com/baseball-swing-blink-of-an-eye-or-google-search-whats-quicker/.

Basile, Don. "3 Ways Graphene Is Revolutionizing Sports Gear." Don Basile (personal website), January 29, 2016. https://donbasile.me/3-ways-graphene-is-revolutionizing-sports-gear/.

"Basketball Equipment and History—Olympic Sport History." International Olympic Committee. https://www.olympic.org/basketball-equipment-and-history.

"Basketball Physics a Slam-Dunk." *Prince George Citizen*, November 15, 2017. https://www.princegeorgecitizen.com/opinion/columnists/basketball-physics-a-slam-dunk-1.23095454.

"Basketball Size Guide." Spalding. https://www.spalding.com.au/basketball-size-guide#:~:text=OFFICIAL%20NBA%20BALL%20SIZE,of%2029.5%22%20(75cm).

Berger, Michael. "Carbon Nanotubes—What They Are, How They Are Made, What They Are Used For." Nanowerk. https://www.nanowerk.com/nanotechnology/introduction/introduction_to_nanotechnology_22.php.

Bhatt, Pooja, and Alka Goe. "Carbon Fibres: Production, Properties and Potential Use." *Material Science Research India*, June 9, 2017. http://www.materialsciencejournal.org/vol14no1/carbon-fibres-production-properties-and-potential-use/.

BizTech Staff. "New Technology Strives to Make Sports Safer for Players." *BizTech*, October 11, 2018. https://biztechmagazine.com/article/2018/10/new-technology-strives-make-sports-safer-players.

"Blood, Sweat and Data." *Atlantic*. https://www.theatlantic.com/sponsored/ibm-how-technology-transforms/blood-sweat-and-data/164/.

Cain, Fraser. "Weight on the Moon." *Universe Today*, October 9, 2008. https://www.universetoday.com/20338/weight-on-the-moon/#:~:text=Your%20weight%20on%20the%20Moon,the%20scales%20at%20200%20pounds.

Case, Jeff. "13 Facts to Know from 2019–20 NBA Roster Survey." NBA, November 1, 2019. https://www.nba.com/article/2019/11/01/2019-20-nba-roster-survey#:~:text=Glenn%20Robinson%20III%2C%20at%206,each%20team%20in%20the%20league.

Chang, Chia-Yu, Der-Shin Ke, and Jen-Yin Chen. "Essential Fatty Acids and Human Brain." *Acta Neurologica Taiwanica*, U.S. National Library of Medicine, December 2009. https://www.ncbi.nlm.nih.gov/pubmed/20329590.

Cheng, Shirley, and Bob Hunt. "In the Last 10 Years, Serena Williams Has Won 82% of the Games She's Served. Here's How Her Serve Dominates Tennis." *Business Insider*, August 26, 2019. https://www.businessinsider.com/serena-williams-serve-dominates-tennis-wins-served-games-2019-8.

"Children." ChooseMyPlate, U.S. Department of Agriculture. https://www.choosemyplate. gov/browse-by-audience/ view-all-audiences/children.

Davis, Ryan. "The 25 Shortest NBA Players in League History." *Sportscasting*, February 18, 2019. https://www.sportscasting.com/ shortest-nba-players-in-league- history/.

"Determining Body Mass Index for Teens." Stanford Children's Health—Lucile Packard Children's Hospital Stanford. https://www. stanfordchildrens.org/en/topic/ default?id=determining-body- mass-index-for-teens-90-P01598.

"Differences Between Graphene and Graphite." AZoNano.com, May 7, 2014. https://www.azonano.com/ article.aspx?ArticleID=3836.

Donnella, Leah. "Simone Manuel Wins Olympic Gold. That's a Really Big Deal." *NPR*, August 12, 2016. https:// www.npr.org/sections/ codeswitch/2016/08/12/484841513/ simone-manuel-wins-olympic- gold-thats-a-really-big-deal.

Dyer, Bryce. "The Controversy of Sports Technology: A Systematic Review." *SpringerPlus*, U.S. National Library of Medicine, September 18, 2015. https://www. ncbi.nlm.nih.gov/pmc/articles/ PMC4575312/.

Edwards, Phil. "Why the Triple Axel Is Such a Big Deal." *Vox*, updated February 13, 2018. https://www.vox.com/ videos/2018/2/12/16978946/ triple-axel-tonya-harding- mirai-nagasu.

"Explanation of Stats in Score Book." Western Australia Baseball Scorers and Statistician Association. http://scorerswa. baseball.com.au/assets/ siteDesq/19799/documents/ How%20to%20do%20Stats.pdf.

Fleck, S. J. "Body Composition of Elite American Athletes." *American Journal of Sports Medicine*, U.S. National Library of Medicine, November–December 1983. https://www.ncbi.nlm.nih. gov/pubmed/6650717.

"Football Playing Surfaces." APT Sports, November 12, 2012. https://sportsbyapt.com/football-playing-surfaces/#:~:text=There%20are%20primarily%20two%20types,for%20both%20football%20and%20baseball.

"Fungi." Microbiology Society. https://microbiologysociety.org/why-microbiology-matters/what-is-microbiology/fungi.html.

Galic, Bojana. "The Average Height and Weight by Age." Livestrong.com, July 14, 2020. https://www.livestrong.com/article/328220-the-average-height-and-weight-by-age/.

Gallo, Frank. "Parts of Your Brain and Interesting Things They Do." Aurora Health Care, October 16, 2015. https://www.aurorahealthcare.org/patients-visitors/blog/parts-of-your-brain-and-the-interesting-things-they-do.

"Graphene in Sports Equipment." ACS Material, December 18, 2019. https://www.acsmaterial.com/blog-detail/how-are-graphene-and-sports-gear-related.html.

Gunnars, Kris. "How Much Water Should You Drink Per Day?" Healthline, April 21, 2020. https://www.healthline.com/nutrition/how-much-water-should-you-drink-per-day.

Hadwen, Matthew. "4 Most Sustainable & Ethically Made Running Shoes." Better World Apparel, March 10, 2020. https://betterworldapparel.com/footwear/sports/ethically-made-running-shoes/.

Harper, Zach. "In a Shooter's League, 38.0 Percent from Three Is the Ultimate Team Goal." *CBS Sports*, October 6, 2014. https://www.cbssports.com/nba/news/in-a-shooters-league-380-percent-from-three-is-the-ultimate-team-goal/.

Harris, David. "Vacuum Has Friction After All." *New Scientist*, February 9, 2011. https://www.newscientist.com/article/mg20927994-100-vacuum-has-friction-after-all/.

Healthgrades Editorial Staff. "Bacterial Diseases." Healthgrades, updated January 5, 2019. https://www.healthgrades.com/right-care/infections-and-contagious-diseases/bacterial-diseases.

"How the Brain Works." Johns Hopkins Medicine, Brain Tumor Center. https://www.hopkinsmedicine.org/neurology_neurosurgery/centers_clinics/brain_tumor/about-brain-tumors/how-the-brain-works.html.

"How the Football Has Changed Since 1869." *Boys' Life*. https://boyslife.org/features/151034/how-the-football-has-changed-since-1869/.

"How to Maximize Performance Hydration." NCAA, 2013. http://www.ncaa.org/sites/default/files/Performance%20Hydration%20Fact%20Sheet.pdf.

"How to Read a Quarterback's Statistics." *Dummies*. https://www.dummies.com/sports/football/offense/how-to-read-a-quarterbacks-statistics/.

"How to Read Your Child's Vital Signs." WebMD. https://www.webmd.com/children/children-vital-signs#2.

Irimia, Ramona-Elena, and Marc Gottschling. "Figure 2f from: Irimia R, Gottschling M (2016) Taxonomic Revision of Rochefortia Sw. (Ehretiaceae, Boraginales). *Biodiversity Data Journal* 4: e7720. https://doi.org/10.3897/BDJ.4.e7720." Zenodo, June 8, 2016. https://zenodo.org/record/912110#.Xyl3_yhKhPY.

Iwanska, Dagmara, Anna Mazurkiewicz, and Czesław Urbanik. "Biomechanics of the Axel Paulsen Figure Skating Jump." *Polish Journal of Sport and Tourism*, ResearchGate, July 2018. https://www.researchgate.net/publication/326648522_Biomechanics_of_the_Axel_Paulsen_Figure_Skating_Jump.

Kanellos, Michael. "Carbon Nanotubes Enter Tour de France." *CNET*, July 10, 2006. https://www.cnet.com/news/carbon-nanotubes-enter-tour-de-france/.

"The Latest Sports Technology Available to Prevent Injuries." Alliance Technology Partners. https://www.alliancetechpartners.com/the-latest-sports-technology-available-to-prevent-sports-injuries/.

"Learning About Calories." Reviewed by Mary L. Gavin, The Nemours Foundation, KidsHealth, June 2018. https://kidshealth.org/en/kids/calorie.html.

Loot. "How to Judge a Player's Batting Average." Lootmeister Sports. http://www.lootmeister.com/mlb/how-to-judge-a-player's-batting-average.php.

Lorenz, Ralph D. *Spinning Flight: Dynamics of Frisbees, Boomerangs, Samaras, and Skipping Stones*. New York: Springer, 2006. Accessed online on Google Books.

Lucas, Jim. "6 Simple Machines: Making Work Easier." *Live Science*, February 7, 2018. https://www.livescience.com/49106-simple-machines.html.

Ludwig, David. "Why We Need Body Fat." *Science Friday*, January 8, 2016. http://www.sciencefriday.com/articles/why-we-need-body-fat/.

Maine, D'Arcy. "Olympic Swimmer Simone Manuel Managing to Stay Motivated Despite Pause in Sports." *ESPN*, May 27, 2020. https://www.espn.com/olympics/story/_/id/29216767/olympic-swimmer-simone-manuel-managing-stay-motivated-pause-sports.

Mayo Clinic Staff. "Carbohydrate-Loading Diet." Mayo Clinic, Mayo Foundation for Medical Education and Research, November 7, 2018. https://www.mayoclinic.org/healthy-lifestyle/nutrition-and-healthy-eating/in-depth/carbohydrate-loading/art-20048518#.

"MLB Park Factors—2019." ESPN. http://www.espn.com/mlb/stats/parkfactor/_/year/2019.

MLB.com Editorial Staff. "Earned Run Average (ERA)." MLB. http://m.mlb.com/glossary/standard-stats/earned-run-average.

Neporent, Liz. "Why Legendary Bodybuilder Who Died with Almost Zero Body Fat Lives On." *ABC News*, March 25, 2015. https://abcnews.go.com/Health/legendary-bodybuilder-died-body-fat-lives/story?id=29899438.

Newcomb, Tim. "From Nike Air to Adidas Boost: The Evolution of Athletic Shoe Tech." *Popular Mechanics*, February 26, 2013. https://www.popularmechanics.com/adventure/sports/g1101/the-evolution-of-athletic-shoe-tech/?slide=1; https://www.popularmechanics.com/adventure/sports/g1101/the-evolution-of-athletic-shoe-tech/?slide=6.

"Newton's First Law." NASA. https://www.grc.nasa.gov/www/k-12/airplane/newton1g.html.

"Newton's Laws of Motion." NASA. https://www.grc.nasa.gov/www/k-12/airplane/newton.html.

Pappas, Stephanie. "Facts About Carbon." *Live Science*, September 30, 2017. https://www.livescience.com/28698-facts-about-carbon.html.

Potter, Stephanie. "Adidas Energy Boost." RunnerClick. https://runnerclick.com/adidas-energy-boost-review/.

Pouraminian, Majid, and Mohsen Ghaemian. "Figure 6. Parabola Deenition." From Majid Pouraminian and Mohsen Ghaemian, "Multi-Criteria Optimization of Concrete Arch Dams." ResearchGate. https://www.researchgate.net/figure/Parabola-deenition_fig4_319262807.

"Projectile Motion (Theory)." Amrita Vishwa Vidyapeetham Virtual Lab, Mechanics Virtual Lab (Pilot). http://vlab.amrita.edu/?sub=1&brch=74&sim=191&cnt=1.

"Protein." Harvard T. H. Chan School of Public Health, The Nutrition Source. https://www.hsph.harvard.edu/nutritionsource/what-should-you-eat/protein/.

"Respiratory System." Cleveland Clinic, reviewed January 24, 2020. https://my.clevelandclinic.org/health/articles/21205-respiratory-system.

Rogers, Adam. "The Biomechanical Perfection of Simone Biles in Flight." *Wired*, August 13, 2019. https://www.wired.com/story/the-biomechanical-perfection-of-simone-biles-triple-double/.

Rose, M. L. "What Are the Average Yards Per Club for a Pro Golfer?" *Golfweek*. https://golftips. golfweek.com/average-yards-per-club-pro-golfer-20585.html.

Rossen, Jake. "Just How Hard Is It to Execute a Triple Axel in Figure Skating?" *Mental Floss*, February 12, 2018. https://www.mentalfloss. com/article/530735/just-how-hard-it-execute-triple-axel-figure-skating.

"Sacrifice Hit." Baseball Reference, updated June 27, 2020. https://www.baseball-reference.com/bullpen/Sacrifice_hit.

Science Buddies. "Cardiovascular System Science: Investigate Heart-Rate Recovery Time." *Scientific American*, February 13, 2014. https://www. scientificamerican.com/article/cardiovascular-system-science-investigate-heart-rate-recovery-time1/.

Shipley, Amy. "Missy Franklin Has a Body Built for Speed." *Washington Post*, March 22, 2012. https://www.washington post.com/sports/olympics/missy-franklin-has-body-built-for-speed/2012/02/15/gIQAtHT7RS_story.html?_=ddid-4-1588692960.

Simon, Andrew. "The 11 Hardest-Throwing Rotations for 2019." MLB News, January 29, 2019. https://www.mlb.com/news/starting-rotations-best-fastball-velocity-2019-c303267334.

Springston, Jane. "Here Is Why Swimmers Are So Tall, and What to Do If You Are Not." SwimmerPro. https://swimmerpro. com/swimmers-tall-and-short/.

Taylor, Jim. "Sport Imagery: Athletes' Most Powerful Mental Tool." *Psychology Today*, November 6, 2012. https://www. psychologytoday.com/us/blog/the-power-prime/201211/sport-imagery-athletes-most-powerful-mental-tool.

"Types of Tennis Courts." APT Sports, October 22, 2012. https://sportsbyapt.com/types-tennis-courts/.

"Understanding Your Target Heart Rate." Johns Hopkins Medicine. https://www.hopkinsmedicine.org/health/wellness-and-prevention/understanding-your-target-heart-rate.

"Video: Heart and Circulatory System." Mayo Clinic, Mayo Foundation for Medical Education and Research, July 7, 2017. https://www.mayoclinic.org/diseases-conditions/heart-disease/multimedia/circulatory-system/vid-20084745.

"What Are Sustainable Materials?" Rutgers University, Center for Sustainable Materials. http://sustain.rutgers.edu/what_are_sustainable_materials.

"What Is a Concussion?" U.S. Department of Health and Human Services, Centers for Disease Control and Prevention, reviewed February 12, 2019. https://www.cdc.gov/headsup/basics/concussion_whatis.html.

"What's the Difference Between a Pedometer and an Accelerometer?" eOrthopod.com. https://eorthopod.com/faq/whats-the-difference-between-a-pedometer-and-an-accelerometer/.

"Why We Love Polymer Nanocomposites (and You Should, Too!)." Craftech Industries, April 17, 2017. https://www.craftechind.com/love-polymer-nanocomposites/.

Zaroff, Ruthann. "How to Carve a Stamp." Ruthann Zaroff (personal website), Ruthann's Soft Block Carving—How-To. http://www.ruthannzaroff.com/carving/howtocarve.htm.

Zilavy, Gary. "How to Calculate NFL Passer Rating Using a Formula in Excel or Google Sheets." Medium, October 22, 2018. https://medium.com/@gzil/how-to-calculate-nfl-passer-rating-using-a-formula-in-excel-or-google-sheets-54eb07246d1e.

INDEX

JENNIFER SWANSON is an award-winning children's author of more than 40 nonfiction and fiction books, including *National Geographic Kids Brain Games*, *Super Gear: Nanotechnology and Sports Team Up*, which was named a National Science Teaching Association's Best STEM Book of 2017, and *Save the Crash-test Dummies*, which received a Parent's Choice Gold Award.

jenniferswansonbooks.com
📘 @JenniferSwansonBooks
🐦 @JenSwanBooks
📷 @jenswanbooks
▶️ @jenniferswanson